Rooms

Rooms

Women, Writing, Woolf

Sina Queyras

Coach House Books, Toronto

first edition

Published with the generous assistance of the Canada Council for the Arts and the Ontario Arts Council. Coach House Books also acknowledges the support of the Government of Canada through the Canada Book Fund and the Government of Ontario through the Ontario Book Publishing Tax Credit.

LIBRARY AND ARCHIVES CANADA CATALOGUING IN PUBLICATION

Title: Rooms : women, writing, Woolf / Sina Queyras.
Names: Queyras, Sina, author.
Identifiers: Canadiana (print) 20210296755 | Canadiana (ebook) 20210296828 | ISBN 9781552454336 (softcover) | ISBN 9781770566903 (EPUB) | ISBN 9781770566910 (PDF)
Subjects: LCSH: Queyras, Sina, 1963- | LCGFT: Creative nonfiction. | LCGFT: Autobiographies.
Classification: LCC PS8583.U3414 R66 2022 | DDC C818/.607—dc23

Rooms: Women, Writing, Woolf is available as an ebook: ISBN 978 1 77056 690 3 9 (EPUB), ISBN 978 1 77056 691 0 (PDF)

Purchase of the print version of this book entitles you to a free digital copy. To claim your ebook of this title, please email sales@chbooks.com with proof of purchase. (Coach House Books reserves the right to terminate the free digital download offer at any time.)

'My only interest as a writer lies, I begin to see, in some queer individuality; not in strength, or passion, or anything startling.'

— Virginia Woolf, February 1922

'The future enters into us in order to transform itself in us long before it happens.'

— Rainer Maria Rilke, *Letters to a Young Poet*

'Framing is how chaos becomes territory.'

— Elizabeth Grosz, *Chaos, Territory, Art*

'It would be a terrific innovation if you could get your mind to stretch beyond the next wise crack.'

— Katherine Hepburn, *Stage Door*

'Shall I ever finish these notes – let alone make a book from them? The battle is at its crisis; every night the Germans fly over England; it comes closer to this house daily. If we are beaten then – however we solve that problem, and one solution is apparently suicide (so it was decided three nights ago in London among us) – book writing becomes doubtful. But I wish to go on, not to settle down in that dismal puddle.'

— Virginia Woolf, *Moments of Being*

Prologue

I was alone, blissfully so, in the early morning of my writing life. I was trying to complete an assignment about Virginia Woolf for my Introduction to Literature class and the more I read, the farther the scaffolding of college, professor, paper, slipped away from me. I, whatever I is, was aquatic, song-filled, but not only joyful, the salt of loss, too, rose and fell in me; no writer had ever evoked in me such a response; nothing had ever felt so familiar and outrageous, so foreign and close. *The Waves* swelled and in them all of time swirled. For some hours after setting the book down I lay on the floor unable to move my body, but inside my mind my body was swimming through time – simultaneously in several Londons and in many child-hoods and countrysides, in forests with felt edges and padded skies, with figures moving through the air like crows.

It was the winter of 1988 and I was grateful to be alone in the little prefab home in Parksville, British Columbia, that I shared with L., my then partner, and her brother, because I felt so naked suddenly, and my body brazen, blinding, without gender or the constraint of sex. Shame followed me everywhere in those days; I was often – even when I stood – limp with it. I can see it now, in context, a shady, ill-lit place of narrow thinking.

The vastness of the space Woolf's texts had created in me didn't so much shock me as soothe, even as they upended everything. Everything should be upended, I thought, regularly; the lie of propriety oppressed me in every direction. How accumulation mattered. Who had power around me? Over and over again the lack of care for others was rewarded. Those who could turn a blind eye to the damage they caused gathered more and more status, power, and wealth.

What Woolf's text seemed to offer wasn't conventional world-building – like how intimately I felt I knew the shire, for example, a world that takes up but a few pages at the beginning and end of *The Hobbit*; or the smell of the riverbank where the child in Joyce Carol Oates' haunting short story 'The Molesters' plays and how it had mingled with my own childhood memories of men taking me into forests, so much so that it made me feel nauseated and powerless; or in *The Handmaid's Tale*, Offred's thinking in the rooms she is forced to circulate in that made me feel so trapped I sometimes felt I couldn't see beyond my own skin and I threw the book across the room in anger and then stomped on it and then tore it apart. What good is a world that isn't an answer to the one we are inhabiting?, I wondered.

I did not want to toss or tear anything of Woolf's, I simply wanted to sink into it. What was this world Woolf was building? It was 'interior,' but not trapped. It was world-building but not realism; it was active, outward world-building; it was, as Jeanette Winterson later described, elegiac; it was, I thought, 'elational.'

This was the tenor of thought that thrummed under the surface of my hours. Waves came, and came again, but the sea I was in was not unpleasant; I was buoyed by it, floating through the life that had come to feel so mundane and so far from my values, and yet it was not a sea of depression and passivity. It was molecular and alive; it was ecstatic in its interior reorienting – and also revelatory in how I felt about the relationship of thinking to the natural world.

I knew the power of the natural world. I had at times seen waves on the ferry back and forth from the mainland reaching so high that they seemed like fists punching at us through the windows four or five storeys up. I had stepped off the path in the forest and slid thigh-deep into moss and rotted cedar; I had seen the miniature forests of the West Coast, trees that would normally tower, bonsaied by the wind; I had witnessed salmon muscling upriver so thick they looked like a Mediterranean roof-top you might walk across. I had seen anger, and fear, not only in the eyes of deer, but in owls, frogs, the indignant fox.

Not to mention the interiority of my own mind, suddenly staring back at me.

The waves were all around the little house with its basement filled with pot plants. Perhaps, if a text like this existed and was worth studying, I thought, my yearning wasn't crazy after all.

Finally, the cat put her paw on my cheek, then the dog with her nose on my forearm and her gentle, plaintive growl, and then my partner's dog with his howl. I sat up. Perhaps, like Orlando – I had also read that – I had been asleep for some years and was now someone else, another gender or a gender of my own, and time was somewhere else. Perhaps when I went to the window, I would see that I had entered a new world? Certainly, having left the city, we had done that. Maybe life was a series of such unfurlings?

When I got up and tried to step out of the water with my dogs, it did not seem possible. The sea was all around me, but of course, you understand, it was in me; the waves were me. I made it to the door. There it was still. The forest. The trees like a battalion of stewing creatures. The animals launched them-selves, two blond shapes swimming through sword ferns and salal. We sloshed across the yard to the greenhouse where I was starting plants for the garden; we sloshed to the river for our walk; and, later, the dogs and I piled into my boat of a car (a 1964 teal-green Rambler station wagon) and sailed to my sister-in-law's for dinner; the next night I was off to the restaur-ant where I worked on the weekends, but everywhere I went I was inside Woolf's mind looking out at the strange world I inhabited with its resistance to all things prickly and queer.

Each time I rose or sank, a new perspective emerged, an intense rhythm of seeing, a pulse of self and world, now from this vantage point, now this, now this, and with each break, a new point of view, now solicitous, now timid, now curious, and with each new point of view my perspective deepened, widened, rose above, until I felt like an emotional astronaut, an umbilical cord on my head connecting me to the vast collective of animals, people, and trees. It's all upside down, I thought, the order of priorities.

And then, suddenly, the clouds parted and I began to write. Sentences shot out like arrows dislodged from some buried, dormant part of my mind, thoughts I had not known existed burst to life. They were simple at first, as they are at the beginning of *The Waves*, a series of *I see* statements that evolved into longer sentences that offered a contrasting and complex portrait, I thought, of the essence of the text. They collided with a selection of quotes from Woolf, questions and observations that built, as requested for my English assignment, a 'conception of the author.'

The writing was euphoric. The statements revealed my attempt to understand, not so much who the author was in the first place, but how the writing was working, what it was doing. Not that I wasn't intrigued by the author – I was. I knew nothing about the figure of Virginia Woolf outside of her name and that she was a feminist and had written a book about rooms. I knew nothing about Bloomsbury or, on a more fundamental level, what it truly meant to be educated or have a literary life. I was, myself, barely educated. My body was still half inside the McDonald's-takeout world of my youth, half inside the brutality of the gender I found myself in; I had one male foot in the mall, one female foot in a bag of Old Dutch potato chips; one female foot in episodes of *The Mary Tyler Moore Show*, and one male foot in the pool halls and abandoned fields of my youth. What on earth was this place she had created? Who was Virginia Woolf? Was she part Bernard? Rhoda? Neville? Louis? Jenny? Was she all of them? Obviously not, right?

Right?

I reached up and into her sentences as though I were being pulled out of gravity because, for the first time in my life, I was encountering writing that felt organically similar to what was happening inside my mind – but, to be clear, I was not at all in control of the thoughts, or the words; my thoughts were broken here and there with clichés and fawning. Sentimentality was possible. Yes, she was sections of them all, and they were sections of her. 'We are shaped by time and tide,' I wrote, 'exposed to the elements.' I quoted directly from *The Waves*: 'I have lived a thousand lives already. Every day I unbury – I dig up. I find relics of myself in the sand that women made thousands of years ago' (127). I allowed more guessing about who, or what, Woolf was.

Of course, the question really being asked here was, who am I?

I should say that this quasi-experimental 'conception of the author' was prefaced by an account of how I had read an excerpt from *A Room of One's Own*, and 'Kew Gardens,' and an excerpt from 'A Sketch of the Past' before – as I said, hoping to find something a little easier and clearer to say about Woolf – I turned to *Orlando*, and then *The Waves*, which had the effect I begin to describe here. But also, that I went on, as directed, to consult a biographical text as well, but no, almost immediately and thoroughly I rejected the biography – I wanted to simply be immersed in Woolf's thinking, and I said as much; the first whiff of explaining her away I found repulsive. Who were they to say who she was? Who am I? Who am I even now?

In truth I had no idea what was happening then, or whether what I had written in the end was any good, nor could I say that I wanted to know, or have an evaluation of it, for it felt glorious to be in it, to have the words flow through me, lifting me from the smallness of myself, knowing that for the moment, what I had produced was the sum total of my capabilities: that was satisfying.

Having walked inside those books, the way I saw myself, and the possibility of realizing the fullness of that self, had changed. All of my weaknesses are present in this first Woolf essay – but also the first evidence of the energy that would fuel my writing life over the next three decades. The writing of these lines felt sexual, clear, vivid. They were a powerful cognitive behavioural tool, I now know; they showed me how to describe who I was and through them I began writing myself into being.

I handed in my 'conception of the author' and waited.

Chapter One

B ut, you may say, and I do too, no one is asking you to speak about women and fiction, or Virginia Woolf and writing in the twenty-first century, or indeed what it means to have a room of one's own – or even what it means to be a woman, a category that has never been simple for me. Nevertheless, as is necessary in the life of someone who wants to write, I got on with the task, gathered texts and notes, opened a document. Then came the pause, as is usually the case, second-guessing myself: surely – even after all these years I've been reading Woolf – surely, there is someone better suited to the project?

My partner of some twenty-five years did not flinch (for I had, in fact, asked this question aloud). 'A writer known for fiction, perhaps? A young writer? Someone other than yet another middle-aged white writer?' All of which is true. I am a writer known, if known at all, as a poet, or as creator of a literary blog, Lemon Hound, that ran from 2005 in various iterations until 2018. Or I am known for my role at the university I have a troubled relationship with, one where I nonetheless have curated a reading series for over a decade now and where I currently serve as coordinator of the creative writing program. There I facilitate workshops, some of them prose.

It's also true that I have published only a handful of short stories and one novel – one that experimental novelists might argue is conventional and conventional novelists might describe as experimental – but I have, like Woolf (though certainly not at the same level as Woolf), studied, read, written, critiqued, and thought about writing across genres for more than thirty years.

Is that enough to convince myself that I might have something to say about Virginia Woolf?

Not by a long shot. Our trajectories couldn't be more at odds: I was born in the small northern town of Thompson, Manitoba, for a start, to an insignificant family headed by a mother whose education ceased completely at Grade 8 and a father who waded through enough boarding school to enter the French Air Force. There were few books in my house growing up, though there was storytelling – of a thwarted, mangled, narcissistic kind, but nonetheless a capacious thread of storytelling – and a desire to write down some of those stories that came out later in both of my parents.

My official school transcript illustrates a chaotic childhood: I changed schools twelve times in the first four grades and nearly failed every year of my education, missing sometimes a third to a half of the actual teaching days. After fully failing Grade 11 English once and on the verge of failing it a second time, I finally gave up and left school; I had already left home and was living on my own in a small room recently vacated by my brother, until I could no longer afford that, and then I moved into a small trailer in a trailer park several miles out of town that made walking to work for 6 a.m. a constant source of anxiety and danger as I navigated down the hill through Thornhill, often hitchhiking into town along the infamous Highway of Tears, named for the many Indigenous women who are missing and murdered along it, where more than once I had to escape from vehicles and situations that were not safe. I escaped from there to Vancouver, and spent several years living and working in the restaurant industry and living in the West End, until I met L. and moved to the east side of Vancouver and began the journey out of the closet and the long climb out of service. It was a good eight years after dropping out that I arrived, finally, at Malaspina College, on Vancouver Island.

Virginia Woolf, on the other hand, is a genius. She was born on January 25, 1882, in Kensington, London, to a solid literary family – both in her ancestry and her birth parents – and has become one of the most significant literary figures of the twentieth century, and arguably the *most* significant woman writer of the twentieth century. Woolf is known by many, even those who have never read her, as a kind of feminist literary bogey – someone a little frightening, or someone who wrote somewhat difficult texts, or someone who was depressed, or someone who took her own life. She is known as a novelist, but her talent was wider in scope. The quality of her literary genius is virtually unparalleled: she wrote equally well in several genres, including non-fiction, memoir, biography, essay, and prose, and in all of them she was a versatile innovator and influencer of generations. She was, in the estimation of many, a poet who wrote prose and a philosopher who wrote fiction and a critic who challenged the form of the novel itself, as well as the form of the review and the essay, which she wrote nearly weekly for several decades of her life, mostly for the *Times Literary Supplement* (*TLS*).

Virginia Woolf's career as novelist began rather conventionally with *The Voyage Out* (1915) and *Night and Day* (1919), two realistic novels concerning relationships and marriage, the first ending with the death of the female protagonist and the second with a more modern vision of love and marriage. With her third publication, *Jacob's Room* (1922), her innovations began to use rhythm and shape – not that the two earlier novels had no shape, they were extremely well shaped, but it was a shape that thwarted the power of her writing and vision. With her third book there is a sensation at the core of the writing that is supported by, but not in deference to, conventional plotting and structure in the realism of the novel. Despite tremendous psychological difficulties in relation to her creative – not critical – writing, she would go on, in the 1920s, to publish *Mrs. Dalloway* (1925), *To the Lighthouse* (1927), *Orlando* (1928), *A Room of One's Own* (1929), and in 1931, *The Waves* – each one innovating the novel form. *A Room of One's Own*, while not a novel, is at the heart of her novelistic explorations, and it is a touchstone in my own exploration of her work and influence.

Woolf also left behind six of the most engaging and diverse volumes of letters in the history of literature and five volumes of diaries, among other select publications, such as household newsletters from her youth, and single and collected volumes of her essays, her memoir pieces, individual correspondences, and portraits of her through the eyes of her contemporaries in a number of other books.

This barest sketch of a sketch of Woolf is only a surface gloss of her output and says nothing about the magnificence of the mind behind the work. A vivacious, eviscerating mind engaged in so many directions at once and with other minds of near equal weight and force that it is impossible to fill in a portrait of her without making these extended links vivid.

Woolf escaped Kensington after the death of her father, Leslie Stephen, the author of many, many books including *The History of English Thought in the Eighteenth Century*, a book on Samuel Johnson, another on George Eliot, and collected essays in titles such as *Hours in a Library* – to a suite of rooms in Bloomsbury with her siblings Adrian, Thoby, and Vanessa. The siblings lived together and hosted regular gatherings that included economist John Maynard Keynes, literary critic Lytton Strachey, art critic Roger Fry, the novelist E. M. Forster, art critic Clive Bell, the painter Duncan Grant, and on and on. After the death of Thoby, Vanessa married Clive Bell and Adrian and Virginia were forced to find rooms of their own. When Leonard Woolf returned from Ceylon he married Virginia – according to his correspondence with Lytton Strachey, she was the second choice, Vanessa being his first.

Woolf and the Bloomsbury circle widened and shifted and they began to mingle with the American poet T. S. Eliot, New Zealand writer Katherine Mansfield, the composer Ethel Smyth, the socialite Lady Ottoline Morrell, and the bisexual poet Vita Sackville-West, with whom Virginia Woolf had an extended affair and who inspired the novel *Orlando*, which features the history of Knole, the house that Sackville-West was unable to inherit due to her gender and archaic laws of property and estate. The letters of Vita Sackville-West and Virginia Woolf are yet another facet of Woolf's life and work.

How then, in the face of all this extended literary history, could I stand even in the shadow of her genius?

I am not sure where exactly my literary career began, but I arrived in public sometime between 2005 and 2006 with two publications: one, an anthology of Canadian poetry that was published while I was living in New York; and two, the publication of my third book of poetry, *Lemon Hound*, an homage and engagement with the work of Virginia Woolf and Gertrude Stein. The anthology, *Open Field: 30 Contemporary Canadian Poets*, had the run that most anthologies have, but the combination of it and *Lemon Hound* set me on the course of taking up space as a kind of public figure, primarily as the host of the blog of the same name as the latter. Out of the blog, my hound-ish alter ego gained a foothold on the Internet.

It had been my intention to follow in Woolf's footsteps – a ridiculous desire, because of my impoverished education and the fact that essay writing has always been a challenge. But journalism, of a kind, and speaking to the common reader, have always been goals (as well as my first writing experience). Creatively, I wanted to try it all: write plays, novels, and essays, not only poetry. I fell, however, not to essays, but blog posts, and those devolved further into tweets. I meant to write more novels but wrote only one before I was caught up – for better and worse – in parenting and the business of a creative writing department. Or, with capital-S Service and Patriarchy.

A Room of One's Own opens on the banks of a river at Oxbridge (an amalgamation of Oxford and Cambridge) where Woolf adopts a voice that has 'no real being' to trace her own thinking about the subject she was asked to address in the form of two lectures given at Newnham and Girton – the two colleges open to women in the fall of 1928 – discussing women and fiction. In six chapters, Woolf calls out systemic sexism: in the form of the professor, the critic, and the Beadle (a security guard in regalia) that has held up white men and kept women out of education, politics, business, art, writing – in general, that has refused us agency and kept us frozen as mirrors to artificially inflate and keep the patriarchy central in everyday life. She relates the story of her magic purse, with its propensity to manufacture money – 500 pounds a year, famously, inherited by Woolf from an aunt. This sum of money and a room of one's own are, at minimum, she concludes, necessary for a woman to be able to realize her potential. Not until women – and here we include queer, non-binary, trans, and those identifying as women – can afford the luxury of hours of contemplation can they realize their intellectual potential. Not until they can tear themselves from the tractor beam of the patriarchy that invests in keeping them frozen and excludes them from the possibility of a writing life, can they write freely of their lives.

Woolf, in some corners, has been reduced to the phrase 'of one's own,' now used for marketing slogans: 'a room of one's own,' 'a ride of one's own,' 'a dog of one's own,' and so on. But she has also become our Shakespeare, the writer thinking women the world over have been returning to again and again for a hundred years. From the young Ruth Gruber, who wrote her dissertation on Woolf in 1935, to Toni Morrison and her 1950 MA thesis, to the hysteria that followed her nephew Quentin Bell's biography of her life in the early 1970s, Woolf has engaged the female intellect and inspired generations in direct and indirect ways.

This includes Elizabeth Hardwick's *Seduction and Betrayal.* Hardwick already felt, in 1973, exhausted by talk of Virginia Woolf ('these are private anecdotes,' she laments, 'one is happy enough to meet once or twice but not again and again … '), and Janet Malcolm's *44 False Starts*, which traces the relationship of Virginia and Vanessa to one another, to their bodies, to their rooms, with a more acute reading of the painter's life than of the writer's, and which, in typical Malcolm fashion, includes commentary on the criticism (and biographies) of Bloomsbury. There are many essays on the room. Novelist Rachel Cusk asks, 'A woman with a room and money will be free to write – but to write what?' and as for women's writing, 'How can we know what women's writing is?' (167). There are Jeanette Winterson's novels – taking a page from *Orlando*, no doubt – and the luscious essays in *Art Objects* that engage more directly with Woolf's oeuvre. There is Jacqueline Rose's essay/review 'Smashing the Teapots,' in which she begins to trace out the contours and privileges of Woolf's feminism. (Woolf's class and privilege can be bracing, as can her colonial perspective.) There is love for Woolf and interrogation and swipe-taking: Katherine Mansfield's pet word for Virginia and Vanessa was *tangi*, the Maori word for wailers at a funeral. There are many strands of necessary critique – Alice Walker in *In Search of Our Mothers' Gardens* asking what owning a room might mean to writers who did not own their bodies. And what of those who don't have a roof, let alone a room? Adrienne Rich's revelations in 'When We Dead Awaken: Writing as Re-Vision' about rereading Woolf's *AROOO* and seeing her writhing, painfully, trying to accommodate the male gaze as she directs her words to women.

In 2006 Susan Gubar, the feminist scholar and co-editor of the first ever Norton Anthology of Literature by Women, a text that had for many, myself included, a transformative effect with its publication in 1985, offered up a revisioning of *A Room of One's Own*. It seems every generation has its revisiting, its cursory glances, its new editions – a whole series of introductions to her novels edited by the Woolf scholar Mark Hussey appeared in the early 2000s. Now there's Lauren Groff's recent introduction to *Night and Day*, Elisa Gabbert's introduction to *The Voyage Out*, and Sheila Heti's essay 'A Shadow Shape,' a response to Woolf's essay 'How Should One Read a Book?' I could have a room of books that are in conversation with *A Room of One's Own* alone (my research assistant counted twenty-three adaptations of the book by 2019). In other words, if you're a woman who has written in English in the last hundred years, you have come through Woolf and have at least some cursory thoughts on her work – if this year is any indication, you've written at least a paragraph about her.

This is not a complaint. I have not read too much of what people think about Woolf, nor have I seen too many adaptations. If anything, I want more. What does Michaela Coel, the young actor and writer of *I May Destroy You*, have to say? And what of my students? I want to hear all their thoughts about Woolf, I think, running my hand along the shelves, past the criticism and biography, toward the fan fiction (here she is a spy) and the adaptations (here is Edna O'Brien's play about Woolf), here a brilliant reimagining by UK multi-media artist Kabe Wilson titled *Of One Woman Or So* by 'Olivia N'Gowfri,' a work of anagrams (rearranging the original text of AROOO to create a new work) to tell the story of a young mixed-race girl going to Cambridge University to study English Literature. And there's no sign of stopping: the *New Yorker* has been obsessed with all things Woolf during this pandemic – pieces from Michael Cunningham, Jenny Offill on *Mrs. Dalloway*, Kamran Javadizadeh on how Woolf kept her brother alive in texts, Summer Pierre on *Love Letters: Vita and Virginia*, and an excerpt from the highly anticipated *The Annotated Mrs. Dalloway*, by the ubiquitous young critic Merve Emre.

Although worry over a saturation of Woolf in the literary landscape has loomed large in my mind since the spectacular adaptation of Cunningham's novel, *The Hours*, featuring Nicole Kidman as Virginia Woolf, I realize that this comes from an idea of scarcity and market rather than joy and love of the work itself and what people make of it. I only recently caught up with the adaptation of Eileen Atkins' 1992 stage play *Vita & Virginia* for the screen, with Elizabeth Debicki's electrifying portrayal of a towering, propulsive Virginia Woolf. Now Atkins, Redgrave, Kidman, and Debicki float in my mind when I think of Woolf. And that is intimidating.

The ways in which Woolf and AROOO have entered into cultural discourse are so numerous and the innovations so bold that surely all has been said and by better minds – cleverer minds, better educated minds – and yet, I reasoned, I have my thoughts too. And no other mind, however brilliant, however new, however seasoned, seemed particularly well suited to describing my own relationship to Woolf.

Among her observations about Woolf, Toni Morrison, a writer of equal power and influence and significance, notes in her thesis, 'Virginia Woolf's and William Faulkner's treatment of the alienated,' that 'Clarissa (Dalloway) conducts her relationships with people under the assumption that everyone is sealed in a semi-transparent envelope, and that the great necessity in life is to respect the envelope.' Further, she argues that 'to live in the privacy of self, remain apart from others … is her conception of an essential independence without which life is meaningless' (Morrison 7).

This respecting of the envelope has many meanings: respect for boundaries, seeing each human individually, but it's also about not coming to conclusions, about remaining open to the fullness of possibility contained in each of us, and in each moment. To see people as who they really are. To feel their individuality, their humanity burning in their faces. I see this as linked to my relationship to doubt, or, as some might say, to a philosophy of openness, or, as writer Lyn Hejinian has written of her prose practice, to a rejection of closure (which I also read as refusal to judge). These envelopes I think of as kinds of ambient, sentient, mobile rooms.

According to Morrison, Woolf's creation of Clarissa Dalloway illustrates an expansive humanity; doubts about the rituals of the world are essential to a humane world. Doubts are another way of illustrating this particular quality of creative response that Woolf's writing elicits: that of not only representing alienation and interdependence, but of celebrating it in the continual questioning and opening up, of not making concrete, of not coming to the text with an attitude of knowing and a will to master, but of radical reception. Morrison's quote and the idea of the bubble come up again and again in Woolf's writing (like being inside a grape, she notes in 'A Sketch of the Past,' pressing against a membrane, a pane of privilege on the one hand, and the enclosure of childhood on the other).

As I said before, Woolf is in the air, and was even before I first read her back in 1988. She was in the gleam of Elizabeth Taylor's boozy eye in the title of Albee's famous play turned movie that offered a slant warning about the power of the academy and the madness of women. *A Room of One's Own* was on the shelf in the home I shared with L., my partner at the time of my discovering Woolf. L. was a carpenter who read obsessively, albeit primarily mysteries. There was a feminist literary journal titled *Room*, a fact that caused even well-meaning professors of the time stress for its seemingly backward and reverse discriminatory practice of publishing women only; thus, rather than insisting on space for women's voices in general discourse, it set women apart, they said. In general, the titular phrase and the ideas behind Woolf's essays laced our conversations and lives, particularly in a lesbian feminist life of a certain generation having come of age in the 1970s. So too did a materialist approach to feminism: all women and youth – many people I knew were working directly with women and youth in crisis – needed a roof over their heads, food, healthcare, including access to abortion, and, moreover, independence.

I was not quite that generation, but I was shaped by them. The women I was surrounded by then were born in the early 1950s. I was born in the early 1960s, in the small gap between the baby boomers and Gen X. I had grown up thinking feminism was both necessary and a given, having glimpsed not in books but on television the power and directness of figures like Maude (Bea Arthur), Rhoda (Valerie Harper), Mary Tyler Moore, Cher, Gloria Steinem, etc. Feminism was in the world, and in our language.

The women in my mother's world had a kind of fierceness to them, as did my mother, though they were far from equal, and, in reality, had a very problematic relationship to the idea of equality in the first place. They were, like my mother, largely uneducated, what she might call hardscrabble. My mother spoke more like a character from Edna Ferber and George S. Kaufman's *Stage Door*, fast and dirty. They had men in prison, they were trying to make rent. They bought and sold things from pawnshops and in seedy bars while their children – me, for instance – waited out in the car. They, and their men, had habits they were trying to quit. They weren't well read. My mother was poorly educated and could hardly spell, but she loved a good story. In any case, why punctuate when you could go on and on? She met these women at bingo, or in cafes where she spent afternoons smoking. They used their femininity as a tool and might say they couldn't afford to have feminist thoughts, at least when those thoughts challenged comfort zones. They said things to their sons like 'don't have sex with the woman you're going to marry.' They practised selective feminism. White feminism, as we have come to understand it. Which is all to say that, as a child and a teenager, I had the idea of feminism, the idea of equality, if not the reality.

There were few books in my home in the early years. Still, like feminism, writing too, for reasons not entirely clear to me, was a given. I wanted to 'be' a writer, not only wanting to write, but believing – as many of you do who are picking up this book believe for yourselves – that I would write, even though I had no idea what that meant in practical terms (What form would the writing take? For whom would I write it?), or how I would accomplish this (learn the skills), because while I wanted to write, the reality of my childhood was that I nearly failed every year of my education and my relationship with English – my mother tongue – has never been easy, or fluid.

Still, somehow, before I could write my own sentences, I set up a desk area on the coffee table in the living room and proceeded to have my siblings read words aloud from the newspaper which I then cut out and used to make sentences of my own. Where did the idea of the desk come from? I can count on one hand the books I had been exposed to by then. I can't even think where – aside from a trip to the doctor perhaps, which was often – I would have seen a desk. There was no bookshelf in any room in any house I lived in until I was fifteen and brought one in myself. My father painted it pink. There were few books on that shelf, but it was a significant moment.

When I did begin to write for money – also at fifteen when I began to work for the local paper – the copy was always marked with so many corrections that the typesetters would rush up from the bowels of the press room, my copy, with its red scratches across every page, in hand, screaming at the editor. They were not wrong, the typesetters: it would be decades before I truly learned to compose sentences, and even now I can't say what makes them right other than they do or do not feel right to me. What gave me leave to feel I could write for the newspaper? Let alone a poem, or a story, or a novel, when I was aware of how difficult even the simplest form of sentence was? Mixed in with my doubt was obviously a confidence, a sense that I had something to say that was not – anywhere I could see – being said.

Here I would like to write about Woolf while speaking only for myself, to outline something that has been a kind of engine burning in my mind that I have tried to grasp and communicate, first in the 'conception of the author' essay I discussed writing in this prologue, and then in a variety of essays and poems throughout my undergraduate and graduate years. I tried again in my third book, *Lemon Hound* (Coach House, 2006), where I trace out the influences Woolf has had on my work and illuminate the questions lingering there in relation to the evolution of women's writing. I tried again at a conference in New York, at CUNY in 2009, gathering, this time, some thoughts in relation to the central metaphor of the room and its impact on women's thinking and conceptual writing. I tried again in 2014, writing from my basement room in Montreal for a talk at the Poetry Foundation in Chicago on the occasion of the twenty-seventh annual International Virginia Woolf Society conference at Northwestern, and in celebration of my chapbook *The Waves*, composed of marginalia from Woolf's holograph manuscript and made by a group of students in the Book Making program at Columbia College, Chicago, the year before.

All these attempts helped me understand Woolf's texts and myself in relation to Woolf and Woolf's texts in relation to the world, and the world in relation to literature, and the possibilities of literature to provide solace, guidance, self-reflection, direction.

Which is likely why, in 2018, I thought it was a good time to revisit Woolf's *AROOO* and interrogate the questions raised over the course of the six chapters and see how the literary lives of women have changed: Are the conclusions drawn still relevant ninety years after publication? Is the metaphor of the room oversaturated to the point of meaninglessness? Can we take seriously these revelations coming from a colonial mind as relevant in the twenty-first century? And what about the 500 pounds? Isn't that an argument for universal basic income? How, in short, in this moment of literary revolution, in the middle of a global existential crisis, does the book hold up?

And how do I?

Let's call him Professor Norton, the man who taught the Introduction to English Literature class and who tried to fail my 'conception of the author' assignment about Virginia Woolf, then, more generously, tried to have me redo it, and then thought better, giving it a B because while it was 'wrong' it also had some 'effective writing.' I was not sure how I felt about the grade, per se; a B was a new reality for me then. My professors, on the other hand, were very sure: grades, they informed me, meant something. Grades meant money and open doors.

I am shortcutting my trajectory in order to get to this moment: on the heels of a year of preparatory college where I earned no better than a C, I had, at Malaspina, begun to actually learn to write, and my grades had soared. This class aside. I was unsure about complaining, but what harm could come of speaking up for myself? I finally arrived at Professor Norton's cramped little office, with its timid slice of sunlight cutting through the glass transom over the door, and handed back my essay with his comments and the B.

He took the essay and sat, first, hunched over it: now formulating words, now swallowing them back, then leaning back on his chair so far that it looked as though he might fall over. Some men chew gravel, I thought, watching him mutter. I could see he was upset. But then again, he always looked upset when I was in sight, or, as a fellow student had observed, when *any* woman was in sight. He vibrated a little, not visibly, really, but for the slight shaking of my paper. I began to feel bad about pressing him.

Professor Norton was not exactly menacing, nor did he seem intentionally mean. He was what might be called 'affable,' and he was eager to be relatable. He liked to attach medieval tendencies to sports metaphors and manly writers such as Hemingway.

But for his female students he was not a benign figure. While it is often the feelings of female students that keep us from speaking up – as in we're having too many feelings – it was Professor Norton's feelings that dominated. His reading of my essay felt quite personal, as though he were lifting every sentence, turning it over, and finding it wanting or meaningless, or both, and setting it on a pile with the rest of the discarded bones.

With every scan of his eyes across the page, tiny darts pricked my skin. I sat, thinking of other such moments in other such offices in other such schools over the years, now regretting the moment I had created. After all, I had had my breakthrough; whether my 'conception of the author' fit into his grading criteria was irrelevant.

For many years after, when I thought of this incident, I thought that there were still some weeks to go in English 201, the second half of the survey course in which I discovered Woolf. Now, pulling out the essay in question from a box of old files, I see that the date submitted is actually near the end of term.

I remembered, too, that it was my women's studies professor who had urged me to bring the conflict up to the surface. For conflict it was. And I remember now that I had stopped attending Professor Norton's class because I was so distraught by his behaviour, another fact I had forgotten until I took a closer look at notes in my journal around this time. And I was not alone in my experiences with Professor Norton, as a woman on this campus. More than one professor, and more than one student, had told me that I had a duty to assert myself, particularly as this young professor was about to be granted tenure. I had no idea what tenure was, or what it meant. No consequences, they said. That's what tenure means. Impossible to dislodge!

I had lived in the failure zone where education was concerned for so long I assumed it was my grammatical errors that had sunk me, but it was not my grammatical shortcomings that seemed to be the problem in this instance. In fact, there were very few grammatical errors because, thanks to my composition instructor, I had been building a list of my errors and slowly undoing them, working back and trying to eradicate them. People who come to language by trial and error rather than by a fundamental grasp of grammatical systems generally do not learn those systems in the way a native speaker and writer of that language naturally assumes. I still have not. My teachers were constantly suggesting that I was an ESL student. What they meant, I realize, was that I had grown up outside of my own language.

I was always extremely hurt by being described this way, but the effort it took to compose a sentence was a truth I could not deny. I could improve – I would improve – but the errors I made were so deeply ingrained in me that, when I felt free, I tended toward those initial errors all over again. The best I could hope for – until I encountered Woolf, that is – was to doggedly track and try to eradicate these errors one by one, which I had done, and found some success. I was never going to have the benefit of pure, fluid sentences that so many around me took for granted – at least, not consistently – and in terms of Woolf, I would never reach the hem of her garment.

On the other hand, as my composition instructor would say, anyone can learn to write a grammatically correct sentence, but not everyone can make a sentence live.

What makes a sentence live? 'Woolf's words are cells of energy,' Jeanette Winterson argues in *Art Objects*. They sing. They follow a rhythm, not conventional logic, and yet the rhythm is also logical. Clear. Queer. These sentences I was writing were not conventional sentences found in conventional essays. Still, it seemed to me that the problem was more content than style. The essay was confident. I was becoming more confident. And I was confident in my unknowing. What is form? What is gender? Who is male? What is stable? What is narrative? Why an arc? Why was it I had to wait until the end of a two-semester survey course to encounter a woman writer? In the world of Woolf, curiosity and expansiveness trumped facts and a punitive reading of orderly procession and here, in curiosity and wonder rather than fact and rule, I felt great comfort. I was elated while writing the essay. I had never felt more alive.

Furthermore, I was present not only in these sentences, but in my body while writing them, and after a long expanse of silence, I had begun speaking up in class. Asking questions. I thought perhaps they were bad questions, because for some reason Professor Norton did not answer them; nor could he make eye contact when I spoke to him, or him to me. He paused, looking down at the floor, or across at the chalkboard. He gave the appearance of listening when one of us (women) managed to lob a question over the net, and then he would shoot a retort to the row of cap boys who would share a laugh with him, and on he proceeded.

But, having written these sentences I seem to have found a way to feel strength, to honour myself, and to begin to describe what I was experiencing. And what I was experiencing, I began to see, was a kind of ongoing erasure. Furthermore, I realized, it had been ongoing all my life. I felt Professor Norton's loathing most keenly, but I wasn't sure it was personal. The way his gaze bounced off me was at once exhilarating – apparently, I had some kind of power after all – and depressing. I was there to learn, not to be liked or disliked, and despite his reactions to me, I had no real power in the situation. Except, maybe, words. And it turned out later, rhythm.

Of words, Woolf has a lot to say. 'All we can think about them,' she writes in her 1937 lecture 'Words Fail Me,' is that 'they seem to like people to think & feel before they use them.' Looking through drafts of sections of this very essay I'm writing now I feel similarly; it's an ongoing struggle to cut through the already written, the already thought. And yet I had done it in some small way in my little Woolf essay, a breakthrough moment of great joy that Professor Norton held at arm's length, as if it might burst into flames.

For years before and after, it was my 'feelings' that I was constantly ashamed of in my memory of this occasion. My reactions. My lack of filter. My lack of self-containment. My lack of social skills. 'They seem pathologically incapable of arguing for themself,' someone wrote of me once in a social media post. I'm not sure *incapable* is right, I thought when I encountered that, but for sure, for many years, and in many circumstances, I was unwilling.

But as Woolf, in relation to the academy, concludes: 'Great bodies of people are never responsible for what they do. They are driven by instincts which are not within their control. They too, the patriarchs, the professors, had endless difficulties, terrible drawbacks to contend with. Their education had been in some ways as faulty as my own … ' (AROOO, 38). In general I agree with this perspective and try to maintain it.

I thought it was ironic that it was the fact of my feelings in my text that seemed to be one of the problems – feelings, the overly personal – and that was no doubt true. But I also noticed how often the opposite was true, as it was in this case, when all the feelings in the interaction seemed to be writhing through Professor Norton's body *at me*, not the other way around.

I doubt any of this was at all visible to the young men who sat oblivious in class, completely comfortable with receiving all his attention, having all their questions thoroughly considered and answered, having all the laughs, as if there were no one else in the room.

These realizations were like a constant low-grade whistle of pain and confusion that only women and queers could hear.

Joanne, a fellow student who had taken me under her wing, was a very driven single mother whose blue eyes shone like large wet diamonds out of a face made of chiselled alabaster and set in a turbulence of black hair the height and shape of a Restoration wig. She was fierce. She was not interested in bolstering anyone's ego. She was returning to school in search of a way to earn a living while being a good parent to her daughter. She was in both the survey course and a class on utopian literature that was even more clarifying and fortifying than the women's studies class. We often had coffee together afterward. She was always joyously enraged. It was aerobic for her. Professor Norton's anger rolled off her like water off a duck, she said, and this was a skill I had to learn.

'You feel things deeply,' she said after a particularly triggering class discussion. 'It will make you a good writer, but it can also be difficult to witness and, no doubt, difficult to live inside – you have to learn to contain it, to give yourself a little distance from it.'

I should be clear too, that when I say doubt, even self-doubt, on some level I feel that this is a noble quality of writing that can – if not held in check – become a negative. But beyond the surface writhing, there is in me an absolute lack of self-doubt. There is a bedrock of confidence that I have something to say. And a complete willingness to say it. And defend it. Leather strap. Tongue lash. Brute fists. Or failing grade. It's only that sometimes I lose access to that bedrock.

We had come full circle, Professor Norton and I. I felt myself slipping back into a feeling of smallness the longer I sat in the little chair. Tension pinged between us.

I have since been on the other side of the desk with students protesting grades. Once, a student – who later wrote a damning portrait of me in an essay on the toxic silence of the university (she was not wrong) – came half a dozen times to my office to protest the A she received from me, wanting, instead, an A+. I gave her the grade she earned according to my elaborate grading rubric, but she was determined to prove otherwise. I was flummoxed. And proceeded on instinct. Later I learned from colleagues that she made a habit of this complaint and came away with a transcript of A+s and, we say, good for her, we wish her well. What I mean, in short, is that grades can be difficult and infuriating for both parties, and I had empathy for the young professor, even then, as I sat, powerless in my estimation at the time, opposite him.

Also, as much as I wanted to back down (both by just giving the student her A+ and by accepting my B) I knew that the way out of both these scenes was to hold my ground and let the discomfort wash around me while being absolutely present and aware in the moment, which is what I did.

This seemed to unnerve both the people I am referring to.

After a while, Professor Norton looked up sharply, as if to speak to me, then back down to the page with little more than a frustrated sigh.

What is it about some writing that makes us squirm? Too close? Too felt? Too intense? Too sentimental? Too much! Over the next three decades of my life this would come up again and again, along with the issue of unlikeable characters and the interiority of people who are not fully transformed, who are also, not surprisingly, working class people.

I was certainly not fully transformed and, of course, I had failed.

The essay may have been entirely imperfect, but it contained the most blood I had ever spilled. Writing it, I felt like I was flying. This, I thought, *this* is what writing is. This is what I am after. Originality, risk, these things count for something, the professors said. So here I was.

Now he braced himself and faced me.

'The essay doesn't follow standard conventions.'

'No,' I replied, 'but it does state in the preamble that it's doing something different.'

'As I said here.' He jabbed at his comments on my essay. 'While your essay has elements that are impressive, it does not follow the traditional essay structure – '

'I was inspired to try something different,' I said. 'I engaged closely with the texts.'

'You don't seem to understand. It is not a conventional essay. I have generously given it a B.'

I did understand. I was, in terms of administration speak, 'non-standard' and 'unconventional' through and through; my body, my mind, my writing, all were an affront to the young professor who had grown up in the bosom of the institution. His mother was a librarian. I knew this because of my job reshelving books. I knew because I often overheard his librarian mother discussing him, how hard he worked, hours upon hours composing lectures for students who seemed to have no idea how hard it all was on his young family and how difficult it was preparing for tenure and of course how proud they were, she and Professor Norton the Elder, who also taught at the college – a big, burly man with a voice like a tarp that, when unfurled, crackled and bristled and was found to contain entire football teams of young men that followed him around cheering.

'This,' Professor Norton said finally, 'is a B paper. That is my final word. That is what it deserves. Do you understand?'

'No,' I said. 'No, I do not.'

'What is it you want from me,' he yelled, this time pushing his chair back and standing sharply, shaking, red-faced, no longer bothering to attempt to contain any of his rage. He picked up the chair and threw it across the room, and then he picked up a Norton anthology, and then – well, by then, as I had ducked and was attempting to wedge myself behind the filing cabinet, I saw no more.

Chapter Two

The scene, if I may ask you to follow me, had changed, and was about to change further, but also not change at all. It was the winter of 1989 and I was striding through the library at the University of Victoria. Having successfully completed enough transfer credits at Malaspina, I was officially accepted into the creative writing program. I was at a university and surrounded by books, books, books, stacks of them in every direction, and trees, and quiet. And light and air. And views. And deer. It was an impossible achievement. Me, who had failed nearly every year of my education, had somehow made a leap.

I was, by now, five years into a relationship with L., whom I had met on a bridge during a peace march in Vancouver. She was dressed all in blue, contained, like a pool you might come upon deep in the forest. She looked across the crowd at me with a hint of Meryl Streep in her cheekbones. There was something incredibly solid about her. When I found out later that she was a carpenter it was settled: she would help me build my room; together we would build a life. This 'building,' however, was proving more difficult than we both imagined. We were each frustrated by our limitations, both of us barely educated, trying to pull our strengths together to make a future and finding many gaps between us and around us. There was nonetheless overlap enough to not give up. I applied for a student loan that year and she used the money to buy a lot on which to build a house and sell it – hoping to start a business for herself.

We were both dreaming of a year of personal and social revolutions, and it was, for many places in the world, if not for us. The year began with big sweeping political moments: Ceausescu ousted in Romania, rallies in Tiananmen Square, the U.S. invading Panama, the fall of the Berlin Wall, the swearing in of the first George Bush. In Canada, conservative prime minister Brian Mulroney was still in office, and the first Free Trade agreement was signed. Serial killer Ted Bundy, who had confessed to the murder of thirty young women, was executed by electric chair in Florida, but the Green River killer was still on the loose. In March there was a powerful explosion on the sun that, according to NASA, released a billion-ton cloud of gas; the electrical current from this event knocked out the power grid for the entire province of Quebec, where, later that year, in Montreal, on December 6, fourteen young female engineering students would be shot and killed when a disgruntled young man, angry at feminists, opened fire.

L. had helped me move from the rooms I had rented in the fall of 1988 in a big house in downtown Victoria (where the landlady wrote Harlequins and liked to enter my small apartment to check on me, randomly, to ensure I had everything I needed) to a small, lesbian-owned house in an area between Oak Bay and the university that felt very suburban with its rows of tiny, wartime bungalows. I arrived in the house just in time for the winter – usually mild, the mildest in Canada, but starting in February there was snow and more snow. *Never seen anything like it,* people kept saying.

Money remained an issue, though L. continued to help with essentials. I worked as a server at Swiss Chalet – a very low point in my life, but not the lowest. The money was minimum wage. Large groups of religious diners would leave little pamphlets instead of tips. I also took seasonal shifts sorting holiday mail at Canada Post to make it through the end of the year. They were night shifts; I came home in the morning and slept.

Did working lives matter? That was one question. I wrote stories all that winter in the lesbian house. It was old and poorly sealed in the manner of buildings that didn't anticipate snow. I could not get warm and became ill several times with flu variants that left me incapable of even feeding myself. Every day colder, more snow, more ill. L. drove down from Parksville with a soft blanket that I wrapped myself in as I speculated about the relationship between the odd winter and news of climate change, a topic my sister France and I discussed regularly from that year on.

Heat was trapped. The ozone was depleting. There were diagrams of bell jars and wave motion. I didn't understand the science at all, but I understood the severity. Later that year, Bill McKibben's book *The End of Nature* was published and Conservative Prime Minister Margaret Thatcher made an impassioned speech to the UN about the need for countries around the world to take climate change seriously.

In the library, in January, where the carpet underfoot made it seem as though the only thing I was hearing was my own heartbeat, I made an incredible – to me – discovery. I took down one large bound edition of the *Times Literary Supplement* after another, leaning against a shelf in the stacks and reading them, and began to see not only what poor vehicles my essayistic sentences were, but how little historical depth they brought to whatever I was writing. How impoverished I was. Feeling, yes, my sentences oozed with feeling, but they headed off in all directions with thoughts broken off. Woolf's sentences were shorn of material of a depth I couldn't imagine generating, and so regularly, and with self-assurance – here in the mode of critic, both the openness I admired in relation to ambiguity and doubt, and also confidence. Such confidence.

This public, outgoing Woolf was a new mystery to unravel. It was exhilarating to see – for by now she had become monumental in my mind, as well as my daily, familiar pedagogue. And it was she who gave me my insistence that women's writing, in all its complexity, appear in the most mainstream sources – not relegated to chapbooks and small presses that only a select audience would read.

Nowadays my creative writing classrooms include a significant percentage of queer students. In those days, while there may have been a significant percentage of queerness, it was not discussed. This made for an atmosphere difficult to feel authentic in, which made it more complicated to defend against the ongoing attention of people who seemed to want to have affairs in the workshops. Even the professors were busy inviting students out. I tried to remain detached. I was there to learn how to write. I was there to establish connections, to try to weave a literary milieu as I could see very plainly Woolf had done and had continued to do much of her life. Literary life must respond to you, she modelled, not the other way around. I was not the centre of anything in Victoria, but I was beginning to feel a part of something.

L. was intrigued by my university life. The first question she asked when arriving from Parksville was always, *Has anyone kissed you yet?*

In those days, I spent many mornings in bed, ill, and still, when I finally stirred out of bed, I sat with my journal and smoked. I couldn't shake the habit even though I knew it was often the very thing making me dizzy. There was my kitchen table, and then the university and library, punctuated with walks.

When I was in the library I was clinging to 1918, as I am writing this now, in our Covid moment. The question remains: how had Woolf remained so productive, so focused? Virginia Woolf wrote something like twenty-eight pieces between 1918 and 1920 as the Spanish flu pandemic eclipsed the war in its ability to kill people, and finished her second novel. The Woolfs were living in Richmond, still in her post-wedding-breakdown low-stress suburban setting – 'I married Leonard,' she notes in a letter to Ethel Smyth in 1930, 'and almost immediately was ill for 3 years!' (*Letters, Vol. 4*, 151). On a strict diet of bedrest – like the protagonist in Charlotte Perkins Gilman's *The Yellow Wallpaper* – Woolf spent months in her room. But by 1918 she was in full swing, setting type for the newly born Hogarth Press (a project started in part to give Woolf an activity to ease her mind) and summering (until September of 1919 when they moved to Monk's House) at Asheham.

Her first novel had been published by her half-brother, Gerald Duckworth, and her second was in progress. Week after week, the reviews and essays came. It was exhilarating to see this side of her writing life, and depressing too, thinking of the output she was capable of maintaining: how did she do it? My own progress was painful. I was smarting from having written another mediocre essay, and several more mediocre stories, and some poems that felt too easy and on point, and this after an entire year of knowing her work. How could I be so ill-equipped to write anything of value? For now, I was utterly convinced that Professor Norton was right: not only had my initial conception of the author been a failure, but that this failure was only the first of a long stretch of such failures that would lead, inevitably, to a literary dead end.

Significantly, Gerald Duckworth's control over her literary publications was a constant worry for Woolf, and the last such delivery of a manuscript into the hands of the man who had traumatized her in childhood, was also in 1919, with *Night and Day*. From her third novel, *Jacob's Room*, on, the Hogarth Press, which she and Leonard started in their house in Richmond, would publish her books.

My experience with Professor Norton exacerbated the sense of alienation from my own writing, despite the fact that in September of 1988 I noted in my journal that my women's studies professor from Malaspina had passed my little 'conception of the author' essay on to Constance Rooke, writer, critic, and editor of *The Malahat Review*, a literary journal housed in the very university I was standing in, and that Rooke had loved my little essay and wanted to publish it *in some form* in the journal. I was elated, but also suspicious – partly it was the Groucho Marx complex of not wanting to be in any club that would want me as a member, but it was also disbelief. This was too early, I thought. I wasn't ready to be read outside of a workshop. How does anyone know when they are ready? When a piece of writing is done?

I had asked this question to Jane Rule, author of the 1964 novel *Desert of the Heart* and one of the first lesbian films I ever saw. I first saw her, towering over the crowd at the bookstore on Bastion Street, and then, after she delivered a reading that was more a description of her book, I watched as she folded herself down into a seat that looked like a child's chair to speak *with us* instead of *to us*, because it was more intimate to talk as equals, a fact that annoyed me (we weren't equals, we knew nothing, I wanted real information from her). 'How do you know when a piece of writing is complete?' I asked. 'When you have nothing more to add,' she replied.

When would I ever have nothing more to add? So, I thought, the text wasn't ready. I loved it, yes. Writing it was a liberatory moment. But Rooke had likely, as my sister had said of an earlier and similar opportunity following a dream interview with one of my teenage idols back in 1981, told me something positive and assuring just to save me from embarrassment – or perhaps, in this case, my women's studies professor's embarrassment. So, I imagine, she ended the scene abruptly by offering me an opportunity, in this case publication, and in the earlier case, a chance to intern at the magazine. 'People lie,' my sister said. 'People find ambition in young women distasteful.'

'Everyone?' I asked.

'Apparently.'

The lesson I was learning was a common one for young women of my profile and generation. Young women who, as Woolf's father, the literary critic Leslie Stephen, observed of George Eliot in 1902, seem to need to believe in some 'outer authority' that knows them better than they know themselves. Need to? Or been trained to? I wish I had read that line in 1989, though of course I knew from literature, and from experience, that this is what was happening, and what Woolf was affirming in *AROOO*. What was the relationship between 'outer authority' and doubt that led to self-doubt?

Our prose workshop with W. D. Valgardson was abuzz with talk of W. P. Kinsella, who had apparently arrived at U Vic with a suitcase full of stories ready to go, and whose novel *Shoeless Joe* was being turned into the movie *Field of Dreams* (it would open in the April 1989) with the saccharine catchphrase 'If you build it, he will come … ' and it felt like the mantra of the workshop itself.

Never mind the ongoing debates about Kinsella's theft of the many Indigenous stories that comprise the Hobbema books. 'Well, if they don't tell their stories, I certainly will,' was what he had apparently said. Not a whiff of doubt about his right to do so.

In any case, of all the doubts – which I think of as generous ambiguity – what I was feeling was not a 'good doubt,' and it became, for many years, a source of shame that haunted me, allowing for outside – usually male – voices to give me the impression that they knew what I needed better than I did. That they were better suited to tell my story, to subsume it into theirs. I knew better; I knew that this wasn't true. But this tendency is so dominating that even if I was mostly successful at dodging and shutting them out most of the time, I wasn't able to all of the time, and the force of men's desire to have authority and own all the stories seemed endless. It tainted each moment of ambition.

And, of course, it wasn't only men who sought to curtail and manage. My sister's difficulty with my confidence was an issue early on and it remained a part of our relationship until her death. She seemed terrified of my desire – 'Stop trying to be more than you are,' she would say. 'You are a working-class girl, you will always be a working-class girl, you will never be able to write as you dream to write.' To her I must have seemed to be walking on air, certain at any moment to plunge to my death.

I recognized some of the rivalry in the relationship between Virginia Woolf and her sister, Vanessa Bell, an artist, visionary, and mutual confidante throughout their lives. I began to wonder if this was at the root of so much tension between women (white women), in general? How often I would experience the beginnings of mentorship only to have it turn, too quickly, to competition.

It was only years later that I realized, or accepted, that my sister's comments had revealed more about her unresolved difficult beginnings as an artist and frustration at her own lack of support than it did anything about me or my potential. Fear. A desire to be heard. These things make a person behave badly. But she was the older sister/mentor, and I perceived her to have power and insight. Her failure to support me at this moment was, as she liked to say, her fall from grace in my eyes. 'You hold people in too great esteem,' she argued. There was nowhere for her to go but down in my view, because, she said, she was human, and imperfect.

It wasn't that she was flawed, though; I knew she was flawed, and I could accept, even love, her and her flaws, which ultimately harmed her own being more than anyone else. What I had a harder time processing was that I had thought she believed in me as much as I believed in her. Stripped of this, I was bereft. As a young queer body coming to consciousness in a resource-based economy, I was aware of the extent to which I was not valued or seen outside of a very narrow role I had no desire to play. I grew up next to man camps. We knew, my sister and I, how toxic that world was, but it was still the dominant economic reality. Knowing that she, another queer artist body and my blood, was out in the world as an artist – now in Paris, now in Toronto, now going to art school in Vancouver, creating a portfolio, the first images of drag outside of Elton John and glam rock that I glimpsed was through her art school portfolio in the late seventies – made it possible for me to think of myself as having a future.

'I'm not gay,' she said when I came out a few years later. 'And nor are you.'

'I am gay,' my eighteen-year-old self said. 'I am truly gay.'

I had assumed that she was gay because she *was gay*, but she wasn't out. It would be a few years before she would come out and become part of the lesbian community that I ran into on the Burrard Street Bridge during a peace march and had found L. But it would be many more years after that before either my sister, or I, would find self-acceptance either in or out of relationships.

And part of how I would find that self was reading Woolf.

Years later, my sister bought me a copy of *The Sisters' Arts: The Writing and Painting of Virginia Woolf and Vanessa Bell*. That same year, she had a show of photographs with early poems of mine as accompanying text.

The summer I started at UVic, I had a chance to hear Constance Rooke speak. It was the year before her book of essays, *Fear of the Open Heart*, was published by Coach House Press. These highly readable essays are a marvel of precision, insightful, but also always in the service of some larger description of the literature Rooke is reading, fitting into a kind of nationalistic agenda. Some writers might be comfortable revealing details about their personal lives, she was saying, but she was not. There was a scene she recalled that involved her, as a child, in a great expanse of silence, mashing her peas into the ridges of the dining table, and how those peas collected and hardened there over the years. What did that tell us of her? Or her family and how they related to her? People were alive. They had narratives. They were private lives. If she were to write about any of them, she would have to wait until they passed.

I was moved by her presence. By the calm way in which she delivered her sentences. Not a hint of rush. Still. Controlled. Enviable confidence; she rode the silences and gaps in the conversation as if she were sidesaddle in a field. But I was also disturbed by what she was saying. There was, in her pause, a kind of desire not to unsettle. For example, she said, if she were to edit out all the scenes that involved other people – and she had no right to tell those stories, those other people's lives – she would be left only with such scenes as her peas.

Well, I thought, contemplating Woolf's 'The Mark on the Wall' or 'Kew Gardens' – which both take a small object and make a large, meaningful, dramatic world – maybe that is a scene of significant weight? 'What can 6 apples *not* be?' Woolf writes in her diary after seeing Cezanne in 1918, with Roger Fry and her sister Vanessa (*Diary, Vol. 2*, 140). Anything, any object, can be a portal to a story, I thought, the peas taking me through the immense silence of the dining table up into the eyes of the young Rooke, as if she were still that child, stuffing all her emotions with those peas into the ridges as she looked down at the claws of the table legs and then up at the beaked faces of her parents, one at each end of the table like guardians of the realm. I can't say these details are accurate, but the peas are as vivid today as they were the moment Rooke unleashed the images. As she went on talking, I kept seeing her thumb mashing those peas into the side of her microphone.

It put me in mind of an early photograph of Woolf at St. Ives, looking up from behind the enormous figures of her mother and father, seated side by side in great armchairs, and there she was, burning between them, her brilliant eyes staring straight through time into my soul. All of Woolf is available in that photograph. All of Woolf burns through a mark in the wall. Just as Rooke's peas have stayed with me these thirty years.

It put me in mind, too, of the essays I first read in 'A Sketch of the Past,' where Woolf illustrates the emotional depth of the feeling of a childhood bedroom, the tumult of emotions – the intrusions and abrasions, the intense waves of colour, the curved petals of light, the sounds rising up from the garden, illicit glimpses of sex too early, too inappropriately, small bodies existing in such a vast array of genders and sexualities being funnelled into the straitjacket of two genders, one normative sexuality. 'Those moments – in the nursery, on the road to the beach – can still be more real than the present moment' (*Moments of Being*, 67). How did she handle so many various moments? Up in the air, tumbling through time? When did she know a piece of writing was complete? What was the point of saturation?

How did she arrive at clarity? How did she manage the revelations of self, shining out from the core of her text? It was this self I was interested in. How to get at that?

⚶

Rooke's comments started a conversation that included a young literary agent – one whose voice I remember distinctly, though I don't think I ever saw her face, as she was also in the audience somewhere behind me. She was a new agent, and she represented an emerging writer, possibly this was the agent's first client. The writer was an unusually *young* woman. She was a poet first. Her name was Evelyn Lau. She had a forthcoming debut book based on her experience as a runaway in Vancouver who got caught up in the sex work and drugs that were – and are – ubiquitous to Vancouver streets. It was something I knew a lot about myself, having had to navigate away from this world many times, having lost a brother to it, and knowing people my age who had been involved and survived and others who did not, and still others who worked directly to support this population.

The women were discussing this young writer's book, which the agent described in minimal detail. A wave of grey heads bobbed and shook with disapproval and concern; how much were we supposed to reveal of our lives, one line of inquiry went. It wasn't proper. There was always something vaguely powdered and tea-laced in the air in Victoria that made me feel apart, but I moved closer nonetheless.

Lau, according to Rooke, had begun sending her poems to the *Malahat Review* when she was twelve. She was a literary writer. A poet. It was literature she was after. Literary writers – here I could hear Woolf in the back of my mind – burned off all the bruises of life, they turned their wounds into poetry, their enemies into characters, all held at great distance. I am paraphrasing, but the gist of what I heard is that literary writers made metaphor, they used literary tools to create art; they did not *succumb* to the personal. They did not go about revealing their secrets and airing their grievances. What kind of a literary life would this talented young writer have if this was the book she began with? A tell-all memoir would set her on a certain trajectory – she would never be able to write herself out from under that shadow.

Lau wanted – and deserved – a *literary* career, and the way she found a book contract and entry into literature was by *dragging herself through the streets* and living to tell about it. Isn't this why Sylvia Plath published *The Bell Jar* under a pseudonym? Because she saw that story as something not yet *transformed*? Too close to the bone? Something *other* than literature? Is this the women's literature we've been fighting for?

There was a great murmur in the crowd of mostly white middle-aged women. She's too young, someone said. Isn't it better to let her grow into her voice, others argued. She was eager, Rooke said again, to establish herself as a literary writer. But what's wrong with writing an account of her life? someone said. Sex is part of women's lives. Yes, but not sex work. Why is sex literary, but not sex work? Great squeamish swirls rippled through the crowd. Then the conversation was brought back to the central motif: she won't be seen as a literary writer; she'll be seen as a *personality*.

What is the difference between a memoir of one's life and a memoir of one's life in literature? She won't be taken seriously as a writer, Rooke reiterated, walking us, to my mind, right up to the idea that Lau had *plunged intentionally* into this life in order to have something dramatic to write about. I was incensed by this. I knew so many young women – myself included – who were exhausted by constantly having to navigate sex in order to try and earn a living, to find time to think, to just walk down the street some days. How on earth were these women so blind? Or was it a matter of simply not wanting such a figure in the room at all?

Lau was not there to speak for herself.

And who was Rooke speaking for? The question of what we'll do to tell stories is always there. It's as if, on our own, in our peacefulness, we have nothing to say. If it begins with a sunset, to paraphrase Mavis Gallant, don't read it. But if it begins in sex? On the street? In a trailer court? How about in a confusion of sexuality? Of gender? Those days everyone was reading Sharon Olds, who certainly wasn't beginning her poems with a sunset. But nor was she leaving much out. We must throw ourselves not into life necessarily, but under the male gaze; or we must – because, let's face it, we're all caught in that gaze – wrestle our way out from under it. And isn't that what Lau's memoir was about? Wrestling through that gaze toward herself?

'It would be easy,' my mother – who loved nothing more than to live in that gaze – liked to say to me, 'to wear beautiful clothes and be looked at and photographed. Why can't you just stand still and endure that for a time?' 'You would make money, gather it up, and then do what you want with your life,' my father said. 'You want independence, that's a way through and out. Find a way to endure and get through.' This, and when my mother tried to send me, at sixteen, singing backup in a band, through the Yukon, were the only possible life choices (other than marriage) I recall them ever presenting to me. Both were my mother's dream, not mine. I'm a terrible singer and worse model. On the other hand, the latter was a path that dogged me at every turn, until eventually I succumbed – at least temporarily – to the woman who would be my agent.

'I know you want to write,' the agent argued, 'and this will give you a story.' 'But I already have a story,' I retorted. She shifted tactics and went on to narrate the story of a working-class girl from Richmond who, when she came back from Milan or Paris, still liked to go drink at the Fraser Arms. 'It doesn't have to change you,' she said, assuming I too wanted to go drink with whoever it was that frequented the Fraser Arms. It might not change me, but it would shape me. It would open some roads and close others. It would smooth me in ways I didn't care to be smoothed. Or I would fall apart dramatically under the pressure. I knew that I was never going to be able to do something I didn't care about just to have the experience to write about. I couldn't think of anything more immoral than a writer choosing to do things for nothing more than to write about them. Even journalists, who must do things and witness things they might not care to, had a connection to the story they were writing. They brought their values. I had no urgent need – other than to excise the incessant desire of others to impinge this identity and trajectory on me – to go down that path. On the other hand, I wondered who, or what, were they seeing in me that they needed to urge me down this path?

But my high school teacher had urged me out into the world. 'Get fired,' he said. 'Find your way.' So, I did give the path a try. I did stand in front of the camera in lined wool suits and ankle-length mink coats. I did endure hard-ons rubbing against my ass and hours wrapped in ribbon like a maypole with a wind machine to make my hair and the pink and blue ribbons dance. I did have some fun, I'll admit, but none of the fun was the truly commercial business – the fun was a shoot with the beautiful gay make-up artist who knew heels better than I did, both of us wearing long man-dresses designed specifi-cally for the highly fashionable post-gender men of the future, and standing in front of a U.S. Navy ship in port with wave after wave of sailors dressed in white calling down to us. That world was never my world, but I did endure the gaze until one day I saw myself walking ahead of me, down Robson Street, into the old main library on Burrard and Robson. Now, I thought, following myself in through the doors, why does no one clamour to get me down this path?

⚶

Though I can't recall exactly which issues of the TLS I was looking at in the stacks of the UVic library, I want to say the essay I was reading was 'George Eliot' published in November 1919, a few weeks after the publication of Woolf's own second novel, *Night and Day*. The essay, with its cheeky opening line, 'To read George Eliot attentively is to become aware how little one knows about her,' and then, later, her cutting observations about the emotional fullness and excess of Eliot – to the point where we imagine Eliot with a half-dozen storm clouds in hand, juggling them into the drawing room. 'It is partly that her hold upon dialogue … is slack; and partly that she seems to shrink with an elderly dread of fatigue from the effort of emotional concentration.' Worse, Woolf's essay concludes – perhaps influenced a little by her father's thoughts on Eliot – that 'she talks too much. She has little verbal felicity. She lacks the unerring taste which chooses one sentence and compresses [the others].'

Or I could just as easily have been looking at 'Charlotte Brontë,' whom she finds peering out between the sentences as if they were bars on her window, or 'How It Strikes A Contemporary' from the April 5, 1923, TLS, where she notes that 'When it comes to the making of a critic, Nature must be generous and Society ripe.' Neither my stories nor my essays had any of this wit or candour, I felt, nor any of this ability to insert myself into the grand, public structures of thought. Unlike the Woolf of 1919, I did not feel the world was mine to describe. I had no foundation. I was all instinct and desire. Though I was beginning to understand the different varieties of sentences and could imagine them like strokes on a canvas, now broad, now thin, now like a continuous line one begins and doesn't lift one's pencil up from until some marked duration of time passes, creating meaning out of the tension, the resistance of the pencil to the paper, the hand to the mind, the ongoingness versus the desire to draw to a close.

I want to hear more about this person, people said of my stories in workshop. So did I. But what was I to reveal? And how? What did my clumsy sentences tell people about my past? I disliked the way the workshop stories were being built. But so too did the poems in the poetry workshop ultimately disappoint – my own and others. Worse, my poetry instructor followed me out of class to inquire if I was okay. What did that mean? *I worry that you are not safe. Do you have family?* What was I revealing of myself? And how could I write if I wasn't aware of what I was revealing? How could I relate the inter-actions that made my mind what it was? My unconsciousness was my gift, I thought, and my curse. I had to learn how to live inside its flow and reveal it with more control. But in what form? Fiction wasn't working. Nor was poetry. There was some-thing between the two I was after. A way of writing that I had experienced in my little essay on Woolf that I had been unable to realize in my work. A way of telling, finally, my own story. But where did that begin and end? *I worry*, said my poetry professor, following me down the hall, *I worry that your speaker – or is it you – is not okay? Is she okay?*

If you write about me, my mother said, shortly after I began at UVic, I will sue you.

Some thirty years later I pick up the collection of essays Rooke was either writing or had just finished writing around the time I heard her saying 'words bring us into being.' Rooke's thesis, in *Fear of the Open Heart*, is two part: first she rejects Barthes' argument about the death of the author, claiming a larger failure of theory to attend to matters of the heart and second, that in three Canadian women authors (the grand trinity of Gallant, Munro, and Laurence), we find a female version of literary critic Northrop Frye's 'garrison mentality,' a condition she terms 'fear of the open heart' (Rooke 9–11). The metaphor of the room is thus evoked (a room with four chambers inside it) as a potential space of confinement that the women are circling in and peer out of but of course cannot escape. Within these constraints, they try to find their voice.

Similarly, I was noting, and would continue to note, a condition I began to think of as the 'aborted awakening,' in which women can come to consciousness of their situation but can't survive outside of it. And so, like Edna Pontellier in Kate Chopin's 1899 novel *The Awakening*, who chooses to end her life in the sea rather than live a muted version of it, or Thelma and Louise in 1988, who find that they too cannot go back to their former lives, having now stood up for themselves, they drive themselves off the edge of a cliff into the oblivion of women who dare to dream a life beyond the domination of the patriarchy.

Better to die than go back to living unconsciously.

I want to say that I find Rooke's sentences as elegant as I remember her being: smooth and smart, insightful and balanced. I also find it much more accessible than so much of the academic writing one encounters. But the writing, while privileging a feminist vision, appears to constrain itself by trying to fit these narratives into an already outdated metaphor:

Northrop Frye's garrison. The action of 'fitting into' rather than creating a new space to grow into reminds me of the general atmosphere of the writing world I came up into and which dominated – at least in my experience of Canadian literature – for three decades. It was one in which a very narrow vision of what literature could be was upheld by a kind of systemic erasing of otherness. As one of the many 'othernesses' that were smoothed out of the picture, I felt it keenly.

As I stood, garish and raw, I could not imagine surviving exposure to the conventional white light of the Canadian literary gaze. And it must have felt similar to Lau.

What I'm describing may be what Woolf describes as a 'central-ising influence' in her essay 'How It Strikes a Contemporary.' Perhaps this is what people outside London thought at the time of Woolf coming into her own – that she was an elitist snob (Katherine Mansfield certainly did). She was, after all, part of a famous literary family; she was of its language and class and its relationship to nature, her father having come to literature in the way of the mountaineering man of the Victorian Age, her summers at St. Ives, her own ongoing relationship to Nature as being an essential stabilizing pole in her life – the twin columns of town and country on which so many upper-class lives are built. Woolf appeared at parties where literary people circled and early on had her chance encounter with the young new editor of the TLS, forming a bond that lasted some thirty years and that provided a foundation for a writing practice that offered her a consistent audience, a constant stream of editorial feedback and affirmation, while paying her in financial and cultural capital. That income, along with the five hundred pounds a year she inherited from her aunt, allowed her to step out of the long shadow of her father and, to some degree, the long shadow of her gender and the indignities of inequality. At least it allowed

her just enough to venture out on her own and not have to worry
– too much – about reviews, although of course she still did.

⚔

According to S. P. Rosenbaum, anger was not included in the
lectures Woolf delivered at Newnham and Girton in those
weekends of October 1928. Anger was added later in revision.
Perhaps because, after sitting with her initial research, or in the
act of transforming the lectures to the book, she did more
research (in the book she records a few hours only) and became
angrier as she grew in awareness. The revelation we can watch
slowly brewing in early drafts:

Anger:
desire to be superior.
importance   to have
some one inferior. (Rosenbaum 49)

Here, in the margins and erasures Woolf the shadow modernist
poet emerges:

Even from   <this> haphazard
    Statement

Of current affairs that the judges & the che
Cricketers & the   <politicians> were in the ascendency

    Though
Film actress might hang by a single rope over peaks &
Lady—looked lovely last night in <{   }> pale   blue
Nobody in   <his> senses could doubt the rule of the
professor: (49)

The poetry in these fragments, as much as it pleases me, is not the point. It is the patriarch, the professor, everywhere professing, everywhere in control: in the courts, on boards, in corporations, and in governments. The more Woolf notes, the angrier she gets. And why is he angry?, she asks. And now I ask, why? He is still there, at every turn, some ninety years later, and still as angry. He feels his freedom of speech is imperiled. He is angry he can't run his hands up the skirt of a young woman in a department store and be thought of as a man who knows what he likes and has the strength to take it. He is harassed by pronouns and protestors digging holes in logging roads and chaining themselves to things; he has all the power, all the money, all the influence – and still, owning all, having much of the decision-making power in boards, governments, armies, sports teams, newspaper mastheads, making up 90 percent of billionaires, he is still angry, still wanting more and more control.

And there I am, caught up in deriding an entire gender, caught up in an argument that can only lead to the kind of negative affect that will further divide. For it is not entirely true. We live in a time, my partner helps me remember, when two women can be married and have a child with little fuss. And when our child can go to a gender clinic. And when universities – some of them, in any case – are attending, finally, to issues of safety on campus and representation in faculty. Anger may not snatch my pen, but it guides it, daily, it raises my heart rate and the speed of my fingers on the keyboard.

No one can take you seriously with these blanket statements, I tell myself. You'll be taken to task. You'll be called lazy. Having given in to your anger. Even safe from the lashes of patriarchy as her 500 pounds made her, Woolf too writhed under the anticipation of attack, dodging here, softening there. But men make such statements all the time, and with great confidence – even, as I've heard them confess, when there's not a whiff of truth to be found in them. 'I can't believe,' a doctor confided in me once, over dinner, 'what I get away with.' Confidence, like sincerity, is rhetoric.

The literary organizations of VIDA: Women in Literary Arts in the U.S. and Canadian Women in Literary Arts in Canada gathered statistics about gender parity in literary criticism. The first VIDA count that sent shockwaves occurred in 2010. Pie chart after pie chart appeared on the internet in which in almost all cases three quarters of the pies represented the voices of men and a quarter or less the voices of women. The TLS, which had provided a platform for Woolf for a quarter of a century, had to go back to Woolf's time to argue that they in fact supported women's writing. No, Peter Stothard, editor of the TLS in 2011 said, the TLS would stay the course! They would not be concerned with equal representation of women's voices. 'TLS readers would not,' Stothard thought, wish it 'to stray very far from our more important commitment to seek out what was best and commission the best pieces that we can.' Have male editors and academics still not made the connection between 'best pieces' and the 'comfort of minds that mirror' their own thinking back to them seamlessly? I gather, from conversations overheard everywhere, that they have not.

So why do I need to bother learning and draping myself in the voices they admire? Quote the texts they consider important, only to prove their authority? Instead, I mark my own thoughts here. I put my body on the line with my statements. And I pay the price. And there I note, in the holograph of the AROOO manuscript, the last phrase on page 50: 'Nobody could doubt.' It's the phrase that the poetic quote above is preceded by.

'Nobody could blame me,' Woolf writes in chapter four; here, 'nobody could doubt' rings through the chapter like a bell.

Nobody could doubt the anger, but also, nobody could doubt their own authority, which like an invisible shield keeps the white light of truth anger offers from entering the patriarchal mind.

The other morning I woke from a dream of a chalky grey room in which I could see Virginia Woolf standing at the window. She had turned her back and was leaving us. Her presence was reduced to a hard, curved surface – like a large grey stone loosed from one of the many massive churches that are grey, I sometimes think, because they are made of the ground bones of the poor. I am always afraid of disappointing the people I admire. I expected this is what was happening now, but suddenly she turned and I could see how she had aged suddenly, and how vulnerable she was.

In a conversation just the other day, in the real life of a Zoom room, with another writer, whom I think of as a genius, about the many kinds of poverty women writers endure, and what the truth of our anger might look like now, if we, as older writers, let it out. As I said, I think she is a genius, but she is not decked out in awards, nor does she have assistants and a research budget. Those who study and write about her work are often well endowed, feted, but she remains – nearing the legal age of retirement – scratching about for money to buy her time to write.

What is it about poets, a tenured professor says as he leans in, that they insist on monetizing their work? Poetry isn't about money.

How many opinions have I heard about being a poet and a writer in the world? Wrap yourself in philosophy. In theory. Be a humanist, not a feminist. Don't speak too harshly, or directly. Don't reveal too much. Don't be too queer. Don't be too negative. Don't be too positive. Don't bring up money. Don't shut her up, let her keep talking, the more she talks, the more I laugh! No matter what thinking one wraps themselves in, the wave of hatred online when a woman speaks can be crushing. In her book *Women and Power: A Manifesto*, which I read in bed in January 2018 as the Internet burned in a wave of #metoo, the classicist Mary Beard outlines the long history of attempts to subvert or squash women's voices from classical depictions to her own experience of being trolled.

How much energy, as Adrienne Rich asks in her essay 'When We Dead Awaken: Rewriting as Re-Vision,' do we spend trying to outwit male voices and their critiques? Never forget, Woolf reminds us in *AROOO*:

> But what still remains with me as a worse infliction than either was the poison of fear and bitterness which those days bred in me. To begin with, always to be doing work that one did not wish to do, and to do it like a slave, flattering and fawning, not always necessarily perhaps, but it seemed necessary and the stakes were too great to run risks; and then the thought of that one gift which it was death to hide – a small one but dear to the possessor – perishing and with it my self, my soul, – all this became like a rust eating away the bloom of the spring, destroying the tree at its heart. However, as I say, my aunt died; and whenever I change a ten-shilling note a little of that rust and corrosion is rubbed off, fear and bitterness go. Indeed, I thought, slipping the silver into my purse, it is remarkable, remembering the bitterness of those days, what a change of temper a fixed income will bring about. No force in the world can take from me my five hundred pounds. Food, house and clothing are mine forever. Therefore not merely do effort and labour cease, but also hatred and bitterness. (26)

Like most of my peers, I do not have a magic purse. Which is why, as many have suggested, *AROOO* is an argument for universal basic income. The 500 pounds must be universal. One or two female voices are not enough. We need – to use a Woolfian phrase – a multitude of voices ringing out from a place of intellectual freedom, swinging confidently, widely – not only, as we know even Woolf succumbed to, in relation to men, in defence from men, cloying to men, bowing, scraping or working around them on the page and in our minds – and here the patriarchy becomes subsumed with whiteness, so much so that we must argue to break the sequencing that continues to uphold the central figure of the heroic white heterosexual male. But this is, by now, old news.

𐡀

Being such old news, we might think that we're a long way from *Hold your tongue!* My mother, long dead now, is no longer a legal or moral threat, and if I spoke out about the wrongs of the institution at this point, who would care? Yet I am warned by fellow writers that I had best not speak about the academy, or be too direct about sexual misconduct.

What is it that grinds us into silence? How is it that we are programmed to protect ourselves: to embed ourselves in relation to male texts, to distance ourselves from our anger, to make it funny, light? It's all well and good to critique the academy, a colleague said recently of Sara Ahmed's *Living a Feminist Life* (not to mention her most recent book, *Complaint!*), but must she do it with such a blunt, humourless instrument?

Women are always, in life and on the page, at risk of being seen as humourless. Or worse: too hot, too intense, too direct, too – as Woolf notes of George Eliot – full of feeling.

How we speak our truth, or the point of view we speak it from, is political. Woolf knew this well. In an exchange with her good friend, the composer Ethyl Smyth, Woolf writes of her struggle to find a voice for AROOO:

> I forced myself to keep my own figure fictitious; legendary. If I had said, Look here am I, uneducated, because my brothers used all the family funds which is the fact – Well theyd [*sic*] have said; she has an axe to grind; and no one would have taken me seriously (*Letters, Vol.* 5, 195)

Indeed, the 'no one would have taken me seriously' is an ongoing reality anyone not a cis white man faces.

Women worrying about reception? And speaking of being paid is often dismissed as bitter. Unseemly. The way their ambition is unseemly. I know bitter well from the last book I wrote, which engaged with the life and writing of Sylvia Plath. Bitter is an easy brush to have lashed across one. But worse is what it feels to be inside that rank affect, to have anger swirling around inside one and without a path forward, as it seemed when I immersed myself in Plath's world, to feel a kind of insanity of disconnect between myself and the world around me that set off an undetonated well of rage in me closer to shrill and bitter than I have ever known.

No, better to write of something other than oneself. Better to leave the peas under the table where they will remain unseen.

Years later I learned that Rooke had gone to Smith College, where Sylvia Plath had gone – and where, decades later, I would sit reading through letters in the Plath archive, growing angrier and angrier by the hour, touching her address book, a lock of her hair – and that Rooke had won the same writing scholarship Plath won, and that, like Plath, she had married a writer with a huge personality and that she would support his career instead of writing prose herself. And soon she would leave UVic and *The Malahat* to move to Guelph, where she would build a creative writing program that would rise into the national spotlight, and where – service, service, service! – she would found the Eden Mills Writers Festival and later become president of a university. Incredible.

'It's in administration,' my women's studies professor said, 'that women can make the biggest difference.' The pull of service that's always there. Women are still not finding a way to flourish outside of service, a way of putting their own writing first.

Suddenly I wondered if, like Plath, there are measurements of Rooke's body lying somewhere still, in the archives of Smith College. And I wondered what we could make of all the data collected about women, and stored, and made so little of, if we had the time and the peace of mind to re-assemble it all?

Chapter Three

It was disappointing, after finally arriving at the university, to find myself moving on so quickly, but move on I did, having applied and been accepted into the creative writing program at UBC in Vancouver after only a year in Victoria.

The story of my leaving UVic is complicated; for one, the year apart – me in Victoria and she in Parksville – had not worked out well for our relationship, particularly for L., who was inching toward forty (a fate she seemed to think worse than death). So, too, I had failed to find my footing on my own as I inched toward thirty, and now, having succumbed to an affair in the spring of 1989, I found myself in a relationship that was already floundering, and where I had now lost my moral centre, and where I now had to re-establish trust.

Relationships don't end, L. had convinced me when I revealed that I had been unfaithful, people give up on them, and I don't think you are a quitter.

I was not a quitter. Either in writing or in life.

On the other hand, it was clear that I was failing as a partner. I was without domestic joy, L. said. Why could I not be more like Theresa? Indeed, I too wondered this. Theresa, L.'s ex, who had become friends with us both, was a lawyer, parent, cook, gardener, a woman who seemed to handle it all while looking calm and crisp – a young, nineties version of Clarissa Dalloway (though it was Simone de Beauvoir and Ruth Bader Ginsberg who were her idols). Theresa not only bought the flowers, but made the money, did the laundry, cooking, baking, vacuuming, and scrubbing of the floors. And she did it with such flare that one was mesmerized. There were few spaces that gave me as much joy as sitting at the huge, uneven butcher's block in her tiny kitchen in a co-op in False Creek, with light dappling in through masses of trees. For my birthday that year she gave me a framed image of a young Virginia Woolf, which I have carried with me now through dozens of moves.

I took a job as a server in a restaurant in Kitsilano and, straight off, tripped going up the stairs laden with plates, injuring my knee in a way that still causes pain. I was already uneven, and now I was injured and laid up for weeks. I loved going to UBC, though, and I had to pinch myself every time I arrived, walking across campus, very often, with my dog.

I had no room of my own, but I did have a desk in the living room, and L. was gone much of the day, so there I could work. And I did. Still, I could not somehow manifest, out of the bright contours of the writing exercises found in these workshop experiences, a disciplined practice for myself. At UBC I had to take a third genre. Now the tension existed not only between poetry and prose, but drama as well. I had to write a play to get into the entry-level drama workshop and so I went to the library to find a model and came away with Samuel Beckett's *Happy Days* and Edward Albee's *Who's Afraid of Virginia Woolf.*

It was during this time at UBC, while in Daphne Marlatt's workshop, that Woolf began to appear in my creative work; first in a poem with a cat, during the first Gulf War. The speaker was an amalgam of the two of us: a deeply historical body trying to make sense of an entirely televised war, a war of blood and oil, the ongoingness of capital in the face of the first wave of climate change concern.

On the surface, these new poems were breakthrough poems because they were messy in a new way. I was not content with the workshop poems; they were too known, too predictable: the long swerve of observation with a frisson of self-awareness at the end – nothing too provocative, just enough to encourage a moment of self-reflection.

Marlatt, my poetry professor at UBC, was more challenging and elusive. She, like Mary Carmichael in *AROOO*, had broken the sequence and the sentence. She was, I knew, a lesbian and very much out about it, though she was not necessarily so in the workshop, which she presided over with a kind of cool efficiency. I was excited at being in her field of vision, impressed with her work (she had recently published the innovative novel *Ana Historic* and was writing *Taken* at the time) but also disappointed when she too – one of my tribe –didn't seem to recognize me, a disappointment I sometimes see now in the faces of queer students who have found me not radical enough.

Marlatt urged me to use the 'I' in my poems. She introduced us to experimental writing, including the community she was part of – the Kootenay School of Writing, featuring George Bowering and Fred Wah, whose book *Music at the Heart of Thinking* made my mind explode – and innovative women's writing, through the Montreal-based journal *Tessera* and in excerpts she brought to class from books by Nicole Brossard and Gail Scott. There I caught my first glimpses of the Feminist City made available through the work of Quebecoise feminists who offered writing that was urban, subversive, political, and desiring, writing that, like Woolf's vision, took root, offering a path forward. The poems, in which I was both old and young, male and female, teetered along the thin stone wall that lined the seawall, with a cat, not a dog – I rarely went anywhere without my actual dog in those days – and Woolf always seemed to have several dogs. But for these poems, I chose a cat, because, like a cat, the poems I had begun writing leapt out of my arms and raced into the forest, or tripped me up so that I had to pull myself back, and had to constantly be wrangled into some relationship with me and the public nature of the poems. They were not loyal. They did not heel. They were all interiority turned outward and felt like taking the lid off my head. They veered toward the prose poems I would later write in grad school.

I put them in a file and that was the end of them. They were, at best, transitions. I was beginning to understand one important strand of what liberatory writing meant for me, though, and that was rhythm.

My writing life flickered in and out of focus. I had three workshops. I learned the basics of writing conventional fiction in the prose workshop, and in poetry, I was, as I said, being pushed to break convention; in playwriting, I was beginning from scratch. I wrote scenes featuring my mother, and scenes between women, but in all three genres what I was interested in was abstraction, a desire I couldn't yet articulate. In the first year I was excited because I was learning so much about writing scenes, dialogue, conflict, and form – all of which were new to me. But the professor was not able to handle the discussions very well – particularly around racism and sexism. The scenes we workshopped were filled with cliched characters and stock women who served the heroic figure at the centre. In prose workshops, the lives under review were muffled, with flickers of revelations that were thinly explored. My peers found working-class characters unbelievable: how can a grown man still be working in a gas station? Or, why doesn't the female character leave? It was my role, in the playwrighting class, to field these particular questions.

Drama was the unexpected gift of my time at UBC. My final project was a play for Brave New Play Rites, which we took on to the Fringe, featuring four women who come together for their ten-year high school reunion and end up telling the true stories about their first sexual encounters.

At UBC I took several English literature courses that were both challenging and of great value to my thinking about writing. One was a linguistics course with the brilliant young professor Kristin Hanson where I was able to look closely at poetic meter, the sprung rhythm of Gerard Manley Hopkins and the lines – short and long – of William Carlos Williams. Another was a course on religious poetry during which the professor held us, rapt, in his oration and insightful lectures rooted both in close readings of poetry (the key text, Karen Armstrong's *Tongues of Fire*, remains on my shelf) as well as asides about his active life engaging with various religious orders and their relationship to verse. Others were not so successful. I took a course on American Literature from 1900 to 1950, in which I thought I might encounter Gertrude Stein, perhaps some early James Baldwin, and Zora Neale Hurston, whom I had been made aware of through Alice Walker's *In Search of our Mother's Gardens*. But when I got to the class, I saw that not only were none of the writers I was interested in on the syllabus, there were no women and no writers of colour at all on the reading list. I went to the professor's office to inquire. He was incredulous. In twenty or more years of teaching the course – he held up the fraying original one-page syllabus, thin as onionskin from years of duplicating, as evidence of this – I was the only student to complain.

The next class he spent some twenty minutes outlining the good reasons for the whiteness and maleness of his syllabus to the class. The writers included were not included because of gender. They were included because they were the best of the period. When he asked the other students if they had a problem with the syllabus, no one spoke. After a few minutes of letting the silence sink in he said that while I was wrong to ask this, he nonetheless decided to accommodate me in part. In his deliberations he explained that there were no writers of colour in the canon in this period, and as for women, he might include a novel by Gertrude Stein but he couldn't stomach her, so he had decided he could include two short stories by Flannery O'Connor. I had read O'Connor in our prose workshop at UVic, and before the titles slid out of his mouth, I knew what they would be: 'A Good Man Is Hard To Find' and 'The Artificial N – .' I was not wrong.

The academy, I had begun to realize, was dense as the concrete it was housed in. The academy was resistant. The academy was barricades. The academy was about protecting individual freedoms at all costs, but the freedoms being protected were always those of the professor's right of refusal.

By then I knew the drill. And with those two titles in mind, I decided to finish the course by writing completely nonsensical essays in which I repeated things the professor had said in class, and then upended them, inserting random lines from the book covers and reviews, resisting any logic.

In my memory, I received a B for that course, but staring at my transcript I see I received a P, a passing grade only. I liked to think that with every essay this professor had to decide if he was going to push the issue by failing me and see where my protest might go, our little stand-off, but I do not have the essays I wrote for this class and so I can't say how the professor justified his position. As for my response to this class, it took me years to realize how ineffectual it was, and how the only person that had suffered any repercussions was myself.

𐤟

For a long time I dreamed I was stuck in a room, just as I was stuck in my gender. In fact, even after I became okay with my gender and was out of the room, I realized that the room was in me and my gender was simply on hold.

I say the room was in me, but really, I wore it on my head, like a great ship settled into the waves that fumed about me all those years I was a student in rooms where I sometimes floated blissfully but other times was thrown against the sides of objects and ideas that seemed, in those days, to be very architectural, very structural, animated by forces far from the world I was in.

I say rooms but really it was always the one room: my brother's room, the one that overlooked the front of our Winnipeg house, the only house, to my knowledge, that my parents ever owned, and even then they owned it for only a few years. This was the room my eldest brother left to go out to a dance one early November night and never returned to.

I have driven to that house more than once in my adult life, trying to work my way out of it. In my memory I am in that room partly because that room became my room after he died, but this seems impossible. Why would anyone do that?

Still, there I am, at five, and still, in my mind, awake, backed up on the bed in the corner of the room so that I am facing the door and ready. Ready for what?

I was thinking a lot about the physicality of Woolf, whom I imagined always in motion, never still, even when she was ill – despite the fact that we see her in photos sometimes sunken in on herself, according to Diana Trilling, the 'long, tense face at once so suffering and so impervious, the large, too-precisely socketed eyes,' highlighting humour and vanity. She was often, as she describes it, in a 'creative illness,' sick with thinking about the reception of something or the scope of a project. My creative illnesses at this time were more related to content, which could have me doubled over in the bathroom wanting to get it out of my body, or, after a phone call with my mother or my sister France, laid out flat in bed with a migraine, unable to move.

I took to soaking in the vintage clawfoot tub in our Vancouver apartment, nestled in a nook under a low-hanging lamp, and just above that, a window. The woman we had inherited the apartment from had used it to learn painting techniques so each room had a different feature. The bathroom was night sky and clean marble. An actual rough piece of marble was set in the corner just big enough for a glass of wine, or a cup of coffee, and a book. I could have the window open and read and smoke, which I was always trying to quit and never succeeding.

After the restaurant injury, I took a job out in Coquitlam, at a residential shelter for youth at risk run by the same agency L. and others had worked for over the years. Sometimes the house would be upended when I arrived. Walls would have holes where children's fists had gone through. There, too, what was needed was acceptance of anger; or the need to express it. But no one wanted to have to deal with the residents expressing their anger. They had often been abandoned. They were always hurt. Lost. What the teenagers in our care wanted was not unreasonable: they wanted a peaceful sleep, a safe room, they wanted to be fed, to be in community, but have a sense of themselves as independent. They wanted to be seen.

Further, we had to create a space they would want to come back to; we couldn't lock them up, as the parents or the ministry of social services might have wanted, or as much as we might have wanted, to protect them. That summer we had a twelve-year-old in our care who was being pimped by a fourteen-year-old. She slept with a teddy bear, her bed strewn with chocolate bar wrappers and drawings of hearts. When we wrote poems, as I sometimes did with whoever was home for the night, she turned all the 'i's into daisies. The kids wanted to be treated with dignity. They wanted to be able to be themselves, to not be judged for what they had done to survive. They wanted protection, acceptance. Not fear. She made the news that summer, the twelve-year-old. But nothing changed. The kiddie car – what they called the police who specialized in cases such as this one – cruised along, picked them up, sent them to us, they dried out, dealt with charges, ran away, were picked up off the same streets, and the cycle carried on, most often until they vanished.

How did people who survived such trauma ever achieve smoothness in their lives? Equanimity? How did people who didn't assume for themselves the right to safety, achieve safety, let alone perceive themselves as having a voice? As writers? Artists? Anything beyond a basic survival mode? It was bullshit. How could you tell your story if your story wasn't one the world wanted to hear? If you couldn't burn all the impediments from your consciousness so that your mind burned with the golden light of Shakespeare, a pure mind devoid of the unpleasantries of race, class, or gender? This aspect of Woolf's argument in AROOO, that women had to distance themselves from the very lives she later insists we need to read about, pains me to no end. That my life would be of no value to her.

Well, unless I found the way, the right way, to write it, which some of my colleagues at the shelter were also trying to navigate.

One of them was an artist who made herself a dress out of large pieces of text. She descended the central staircase in the Vancouver Art Gallery like a woman wedding her own intellect, a long literary train of paper behind her.

One of the first truly angry literary women I encountered was Marilyn French, who gave a talk in 1989. What to make of a radical feminist in heels and a smart Chanel suit? I can't recall exactly what Marilyn French, born the year *AROOO* was published, read from when she visited UBC. I recall seeing my Prose professor a row in front of me and catching her eye. I admired her enormously, my Prose professor, even though I knew that when she looked at me she saw a body that she couldn't recognize, or didn't know what to make of. Invisibility, or visibility with a caveat, was something I was accustomed to. I didn't give it much thought – though I was right in my evaluation of her regard of me, I know, because years later, running into me at AWP, she apologized for 'not seeing me' then.

See me or not, I adored her. But now I wonder what was it she was not seeing? My queerness? I was generally the only openly queer body in whatever class I was in at that time, even if there were other queer bodies among us. Questions of queerness fell to me — not that there were many. As did questions of feminism. But it wasn't only my queerness, or my feminism; it was my intensity, I realized recently, after years of being ashamed of it. It was a matter of borderlessness, a porousness; my consciousness was at once on the surface, flickering for all to see, and deeply buried. The depth my mind had to travel from hiding to surface was uncomfortable for people. The moments between thought and speech were always fraught because there was space there, in that speech hesitation, where I could be interrupted, or overwritten. So easily. So quickly. A mindless snap of thought. It would take another decade to shorten that distance, to make it through a thought without interruption.

Further, I preferred silence to the possibility of saying something overly raw, or revealing, or prickly. I never knew what shape a sentence might take, what it might reveal, or how to change it once the utterance was out. I realize now how uncomfortable this made people, but I did not know why, or how, to change, hide, or dim the situation, other than to completely silence myself, which was a choice I often made.

My Prose professor was young and had gone to Columbia, which meant that she had lived in New York. She was well read and she brought meaningful discussions about craft to the table; her insistence on conflict, use of imagery, and subtext provided a bedrock. I found her basic directness refreshing. She didn't pontificate; she didn't waste time. She was also from a working-class background. Above all, she was unfailingly energetic, as young professors often are, and it appeared that knowing French was already going to be at UBC to give a lecture, she had been wise enough to add a lecture for creative writing students. A smaller, less formal affair.

I knew very little about the visiting author, but I knew *The Women's Room* (1977), the novel she was famous for. It's a watershed account of women's lives that includes a character who is a radical feminist, a rational enough character who could nonetheless make statements such as 'All men are rapists, and that's all they are. They rape us with their eyes, their laws, their codes.' She had come to UBC to give a lecture – *Beyond Power* – which you can still access on the University of British Columbia's Open Archives, which I did while preparing for this book. The lecture is a bracing moment to revisit, strangely, from a time when we could be crammed into rooms so full there had to be an overflow room, and where we had the luxury of talking about the environmental and social apocalypse we are hurtling toward as a distinct possibility, or even probability, but not yet – as it is for us – a reality. The warnings she offers – of not challenging oil/patriarchy/militarism – don't seem prescient, though they are on the nose, but given the atmosphere they were launched into, and the relatively minimal impact women's rage has had, in general, on decision-making, they seem unbearably sad.

Still, even nearing the end of my undergraduate degree, the stories were *not* coming out in the shape and texture that I conceived of them. What was clear to me, but often problematic in workshop, was the flimsiness of the polemic thrumming in them. I was intrigued by French but not a huge fan of her novels. I had in my mind Jeanette Winterson's *Sexing the Cherry*, Elizabeth Smart's *By Grand Central Station I Sat Down and Wept*, and Duras' *The Lover*. It had always been prose I longed for, not poetry, which constrained and elided so much. But how to be present in it? Particularly when the prose veered off from the common sentence because the common sentence would not do. One could sense Smart from the very first line in *Grand Central*: 'I am standing on a corner in Monterey, waiting for the bus to come in, and all the muscles of my will are holding my terror to face the moment I most desire.' Or from *The Lover*: 'One day, I was already old, in the entrance of a public place a man came up to me.' Those sentences, like the openings of Woolf's novels, set my pulse racing.

Watching French, I was impressed by how she appeared to be able to say so much, and to reach so many people. I reasoned that a large part of this was the package I was staring at. She looked like 'a very nice lady.' She had, as my mother would have said, poise. She stood in the manner of women born in the 1930s (1929, to be exact), with coiffed hair and shoulders like Joan Crawford. She wore blue, I believe, a well-cut suit that must have been Chanel. She read with confidence, presence (just enough – I did catch a hint of boredom, or maybe impatience, looking out at us), and energy. It didn't matter what she was saying, I thought, because the confidence had an energy of its own. Suddenly she was finished and stood a bit forward, one hand on the table, as she braced for questions.

Questions at such events in universities usually involve a lengthy restatement of what the author has just read, followed by a vague question that is basically asking for a different lecture. And if the speaker is a woman, there is an element of undermining and condescension in this performance. These questions are most often asked by men. At the French lecture, one man got a long non-question in, then another, before a young man got up and at some length described his good intentions and his anxiety around feminism, ending with the question of what he could do to support women.

'Well,' she said, 'for a start you can sit down, shut up, and let a woman speak.'

There was a wave of shock in the room.

'Look,' she went on, 'you've just taken up all the time with your questions. Are there no women in the room?'

If memory serves, it was my Prose professor whose eyes I met then and whose eyebrows, like my own, raised with delight, but who, like all the other women in the room, did not ask a question. Two statements French made often were illuminated here: the pursuit of power is never-ending and never satisfied, and we all make the patriarchy possible.

In an interview with Charlie Rose from around this time, French says that she knows there are men who individually take responsibility for their own violence, and for their own children, but men as a whole have not done this. Until they do, there is no hope of change. French laughs later, when Rose asks her when she thinks the changes feminism is asking for will come. 'Not in my lifetime,' she says, with her very disarming smile and an emphatic shake of her head. 'No, not in my lifetime.'

Once, when I was about ten years old, we were playing scrub baseball on a diamond in Surrey, a much-maligned suburb of Vancouver. A group of boys appeared at the edge of the field, near first base. I was on the pitcher's mound and, like all the other children, I turned to look.

'Move,' one of them said. 'All of you. I'm walking your way. Anyone left on the field I'm going to flatten.'

'Why?' I asked.

'Because I said so.'

The children around me immediately moved off, but my body hardened in place.

'Clear the field,' he said again. 'I'm going to count to three.'

I was shaking with rage.

'One,' he said, slowly striding forward.

I didn't budge.

'Two.' He kept his pace.

'Three.'

Even when we made contact and I stumbled backward, the force of my resistance to his body kept me upright. Back and back, I stumbled, righted myself, stumbled, righted myself until I was against the fence and his face was in mine.

'I said move,' he repeated. He was slightly shorter than me, with a freckled face and brush cut, and I could see he was enjoying himself.

'Fuck you,' I said.

Then he stepped back and unleashed a series of blows that made my head feel like a puppet.

I had never felt such force or seen such speed. Even with my cousins, who had a punching bag in their garage and took boxing extremely seriously. My head snapped and snapped against the fence. First my right eye. Then my left cheek. Then chin. Then right brow. Left. Chin. Finally, I regained myself a minute and did what I had somehow been prepared for by those very cousins who took boxing lessons and played football: I put my knee between his legs and pulled up as hard and fast as I could, and he folded, both hands to his groin, looking up long enough to call me a bitch.

The first image of Woolf I recall seeing was the classic side profile, her hair in the bun she is famous for. She had, according to Dame Edith Sitwell, a 'moonlit transparent beauty' and was 'exquisitely carved' with her large 'thoughtful eyes that held no foreshadowing' of her tragic end (Stape 38). Sitwell is no doubt describing Woolf in life, in action, rather than this early photograph, which seems to catch her in the act of coming out into the world in 1902, at twenty years old – two years before her father died and three years before she sold her first review to the TLS. These two things are not unrelated. Had her father not died when he did, Woolf notes, she might not have had a literary career.

This is doubtful, considering her drive and talent, and the strong model of a literary life that Leslie Stephen offered her. Being 'liberated' from family expectations and stress through death is a common literary trope, but perhaps, had her father not died when he did, she would have taught a few more years of night courses at Morley College. When I finally dip into the writing of Leslie Stephen, I see echoes of him everywhere in Woolf, and not only as depicted by the blustering father in *To the Lighthouse*, but also his passion and intelligence. Now I see how empowering it must have been for her to come to books in his library, witnessing his struggles and his rages. Self-absorbed he might have been, but he was obviously a vibrant thinker capable of holding vast canvases in his mind and storing poetry in his body. These are the tools he bequeathed his daughter – that, and something firm and public to write against.

The family, in these coming-of-age-as-a-writer narratives, is often seen in retrospect as having been ideal in some ways, or at least loving, but it can also be an oppressive origin story from which the burgeoning writer is suddenly freed. How many literary figures are orphans who live in idealized traumatic states of quasi-liberation? In children's and young adult literature, the young protagonist often finds herself in a new home that she must further liberate herself from, but the important part of these kinds of orphan narratives is that the child has experienced a rupture. She has been taken out of context and is therefore alienated. An outsider. She is aware of herself in the world in a way that people who don't experience such ruptures can never be.

Much has been made of the loss of Woolf's mother, her elder sister Stella, her father, and then her beloved brother Thoby, whom she elegizes in *Jacob's Room*. The loss of my eldest brother when I was five has haunted my entire life – far longer, and more deeply, than was necessary or is, perhaps, usual.

Coping mechanisms are handed down, as well as literary strengths – they are not always the healthiest, but they often have beauty.

The cat poems, casting my body over Woolf's on the seawall, never appeared anywhere, and I read them only once, but I feel them in me still. The way the speaker walked right at the edge of the wall, half in the sea, lamenting oil (along with climate change came the beginning of the Gulf Wars). A dark swerve in the world was happening. I wanted to be in it and retreat from it with equal force, which the poem enacted. But it was also a kind of wish for self-acceptance. Photographs of me at that time depict my unevenness.

I see Woolf in the series of photos at Lady Ottoline Morrell's garden party, wearing a designer gown and, even in that setting, carrying a sheaf of paper. This is a small detail but the ease with which she literally carried her career everywhere with her was not lost on me. I was not able to muster explanation enough when asked what it was I was doing – but inside I was roiling and churning to say the thing. How does one burst out?

'I don't remember her clothes well in themselves, because they seemed merged in her,' Elizabeth Bowen writes, but the last time she saw her, in Rodmell, where the Woolfs had a country home, she was sitting back on her heels 'in a patch of sun, early spring sun … laughing in the most consuming choking kind of way.'

Where is she now? Bowen wonders in *Virginia Woolf: Interviews and Recollections*: 'Nobody with that capacity for joy, I think, can be nowhere' (qtd. in Stape 172).

'Now that's an odd reflection,' Woolf writes to Vita on August 8, 1931, 'how one's relation with a person seems to be continued after death in dreams, and with some odd reality too.' I never met Virginia Woolf but her joy bubbles up in me. When I discovered her I felt, first, flattened, like an air mattress with the air completely sucked out, impossible – I thought – to continue living in bleakness when it was possible to be so alive. Then to be filled again with something purer and lighter that made it seem like I was floating, upside down in my room, and might, if a breeze came through, be taken up into the clouds if I weren't paying attention, casting a line here or there to keep myself tethered. Having never been alive at the same moment as her, I nonetheless feel how her body moved through the city streets, pressing into the air and sliding past other bodies so that they had the sensation they had been brushing past silk.

At some point during my second year at UBC I stopped menstruating. I was elated. I had always believed – or wanted to believe – that if I willed something hard enough, I might make it happen, and here was one of my most common dreams – stopping the reproductive aspects of my gender's biology.

I drove out to visit my mother. She was living in the middle of the Union of Operating Engineers training plant where my father worked. After making her coffee and listening to her complaints and updates – a matter of several hours during which she used her puffer several times between lighting cigarettes and replenishing her coffee to the rhythm of the front-end loaders and dump trucks circling the trailer – she finally stopped to ask how I was. When I told her about the end of bleeding with some delight, she did not meet it with the enthusiasm I expected. It was not good news. No? No, it is not.

L. concurred and so off I went to see our doctor.

Dr. Hister, whom I became a patient of through L., was diligent, even making a house call once when a migraine knocked me out for several days and I became dehydrated. Now I listened, slightly distracted by a framed newspaper story tracing his father's life in Montreal, as he asked me uncomfortable questions about my relationship to my body and my gender. Was I comfortable being female? Did the hair growth on my body bother me? Was I worried that I was so thin? I believed in being thin. Hungry, because, as I note in my diary, 'if I can stay lean, I can always flee.'

The encounter shook me. I was fine, I assured him. I was fine with who, what, I was.

'Of course you are,' he said, in the voice I often heard on the CBC where he had a regular segment.

'Do you want to find out why it's happening? Whether it's hormones? Sometimes being too thin' – I was very, very thin – 'this happens … but it could be something else.'

What something else? What 'it'?

Was I not fine with my body after all? Did I want to be something else? Here doubt took a troubling swerve. I thought of myself as androgynous. In that I was fine. I didn't want to be fixed.

Off I went to an endocrinologist and then, during one of the intense hours of the first Gulf War, had my first CT scan.

There was a small, benign tumour nestled in the centre of my head, under my pituitary gland. It explained the cessation of menstruation and the hair growth on my body.

So, I thought, I had created a literal block. I was so disconnected from my body I had not noticed the hairs that had begun to grow here on my breasts and up to my belly button? I was aware of my thinness; I didn't need to think about bras then, I could pass for a boy or a girl, depending on how I felt and what I wore, which was usually somewhere in the middle, in a nondescript way.

Was this condition to do with my anxiety about my gender? Could I admit that I felt trapped by the possible ways I could inhabit my gender? My sexuality? My body? When pressed to think about it, I could see no way forward, and so, rather than move forward, I slid, as L. sometimes accused me of doing, sideways, like a crab. I was to be medicated. But, the endocrinologist said, you have to think carefully because once you start medication, that's it, for life.

Maybe, like Orlando, I would change genders as I began to find my way from poetry to prose.

Chapter Four

The university where I did my MA in the early 1990s, and where I now teach, has been the site of several sexual misconduct complaints and investigations. It would be impossible to quantify the suffering involved, the hours consumed, the space taken up, and I am loathe to give it any more air than it has already consumed – even if, legally, I could – because it is the women and the students who carry the weight and who attempt to make institutionalized changes; it is the women and the students who, before and after, carry the burden.

It's the women who navigate the cancerous silences in their own bodies. How many others are there, I often wonder, as I walk to and from the university. How many books interrupted? How many creative lives stolen? After the story finally broke in the national media, I lay on the floor of the classroom and cried as the energy of so many of the beautiful lives that had come to these rooms passed through me.

If I accounted for every time I changed routes because someone appeared in my path or cornered me in a cloakroom, or every time some colleague or boss wanted to consume me or silence me, if I gave an account of my own thesis defence, this would be a tale of pure, burning rage.

⚶

I'm tired of being angry, I was thinking, as I walked through the forest in the middle of Montreal with the American poet

Jen Bervin, author of *Nets*, a book that unearths a post–9/11 New York eerily embedded in Shakespeare's sonnets (and one of my favourite books of poetry). She has, more recently, published a gorgeous book of Emily Dickinson's envelope poems. Dickinson, who, of course, never had the pleasure of seeing her own work in print.

As we walked, pools of time billowed around Bervin. Poetry, it seemed, had loosened itself from the apparatus of the university and was following us along the rugged footpaths that line the outermost edge of Mount Royal, the forest floor already carpeted with autumn leaves, half eaten from the invading moths that signal a worsening climate. Moths that I had first noticed while on a walk with another poet and translator, Erín Moure. Moure, like Dickinson, claims time, and Bervin, like Woolf, claims time. Bervin appeared to have achieved something like the equanimity Woolf emanates but, according to Leonard, never quite achieved for herself. Maybe Moure, who had turned what I thought poetry was on its head when I first heard her read in Montreal in the early 1990s, had also achieved a kind of equanimity in her life, moving as she did from poetry to translation to prose to trans-elation (Moure's way of ecstatically entering her person into the act of translation). And Moure, like Woolf and Bervin, had chosen a life outside the academy.

I was enjoying Bervin's company. What she said was almost irrelevant; it was the energy, a thread that rustled through the trees, around and between us, as we walked, that I responded to. A conversation on the level of molecule. I noticed, too, the silence, the duration, so that the clean lines of her studio appeared; in her movement I could see her devotion to her work, in the sweep of her eyes the hours that build, not walls to keep the world out but a stronger, clearer sense of one's self in context with the world. Time was hers now, sewn on the wave's tooth, with silver thread – a detail I had noticed in her work the day before at a gallery near Place des Arts. Yes, I thought, she was a poet whose mind seemed to have 'consumed all impediments and become incandescent,' as Woolf says in AROOO, that women must do to truly achieve intellectual freedom, which I was beginning to think of, more simply, as an alignment of mind and body.

That is what one wants. A deep connection to the body. A deep connection to the work. Not a surface reorienting as is so easy to achieve in our Twitter life. A quick response to an idea too soon shared. I was certainly guilty of succumbing to this. Despite being so aware of the price. As I slide past the map of writers who have achieved this deep interiority, I stick a flag in the crumbling earth and try to mark each of them for reference. The poet and novelist Dionne Brand creates work that whispers like a bomb you must inch closer to hear. Gail Scott, my neighbour, whose triplex I try to make out for Bervin from the ridge where I'm standing, who, like Duras and Woolf, rearranged in my mind what I thought a sentence could do – not to mention bending time and, like Moure, rearranging one's perception of the world by elongating the space between recognition and affirmation. And Claudia Rankine, too, I thought, as her name burst organically out of my conversation with Bervin, this is someone who seems to have achieved a kind of equanimity in her work and life, and who has moved, over the course of her career, from a singular lyric voice to a choral or scenic ensemble, as we see in *Citizen*.

It was the descriptions of Woolf's writing life that were so exhilarating and daunting, the poet Lisa Robertson said a few weeks later, walking with me in the same forest, with similar pools of time swagging around her: how much she did in a day, what determination, and scheduling!

We are a generation of poets, my peers and I, reaching the age Woolf was at the end of her life, when she found that she could not work, could not see a future, and so merged with the water that had given such deep rhythm to her life.

I noticed I wrote 'career' there first, 'at the end of her career,' and then changed it to 'life,' but I think that in this instance the interchangeability of life and work is the point, and not in the sense of her being too overly identified with work, but rather the wisdom of one's work being thoroughly, beautifully, productively, ethically entwined in one's life. All my life I have been shamed for my ambition. But what has it been for? What have I longed for? Not for prizes, or fame, or bestseller lists, but for an authentic intellectual and creative practice. Time and money enough for work.

Language, stories, come out of our bodies. They are our clay. Our mind the hands that hold the clay. This then, this full-bodied writing. Like Elizabeth Smart standing at the bus station with all of her nerve endings outside her body. And here we are reaching this age in a similar political and social world, the illusion of equality punctured, as it periodically is – politics erupting into nationalism, fascism, and made more difficult to counter as we face the existential and immediate challenge of climate devastation.

Finding a way through war, Woolf writes in 1939, that's the challenge. Finding a way to remain authentic, real, attached to the world and ourselves as it explodes, is bulldozed and terrorized by extreme weather events. That's the room Woolf built. And all of us come through it. Her rooms are, for so many, the first spaces where we let our limbs shake out and where we can luxuriate in our thinking. So beautiful. She mirrors us, or rather, she pulls the mirror out of the position of reflecting only the white, heterosexual patriarchy and places it at our feet.

Where my relationships are unspoken, undefined, I suffer. Where my work is hidden, I suffer. Where – but that's it, isn't it? Those Woolfian sentences I first read more than thirty years ago seemed to come out of a place in me that was a land undiscovered. A dormant self not reliant on male interlocutors.

Where my*self* hides under the density of my enclosure. Through a tumult of feeling, I can hear Woolf, always, like the hum of the land, of water moving across leaves, down bark, through the moss, and I heard it in Bervin's question, too, or assumed I did: What is it you are working on?

If I could create a space for my own mind, daily, is a mantra I cling to, a dream practice, if I could only connect.

It's also the mantra Woolf affirms: connect everything! We see this in *The Waves*, AROOO, and *Orlando*. We see it in the conceptual practices of women from Mary Kelly to Agnes Martin to Jen Bervin: to make women's labour visible, to connect human presence to the outcome of actions. I glimpsed this profoundly as a child, watching my mother prepare dinner: things came out of cans, cans were dumped into garbage bins. 'What is that?' I asked my mother. 'What is what? The garbage? The garbage is the garbage.' 'But where does it go?' 'It goes to the dump.' 'But what is the dump?' How sad this made me feel, all this materiality between ourselves and dinner. Putting the material of the work, the spirit of the work first, not fitting the work into systems that do not love us. These women made art from their labour, Kelly with her lovingly archived shitty diapers. This was art from the service of gender. I have tried to be as methodical as these women in my work, but methodical seems to bring me no joy. Nor, as I find in composing this book, does linearity or realism. One must, of course, represent one's life honestly. But honesty, authenticity, has nothing to do with realism.

What I am after, what I am always after, is a peek into how one lives, but also into the abstract feeling of those lives and the impact of lives on the world. Also, the impact of the world on the body. How to achieve a practice that makes room for this to happen?

Woolf, I know, did a dozen things daily, divided time like a great pie she would eat her way through with great pleasure: now writing, now a walk through the garden to the downs then through the city, now to lunch, now to the press room and business, now to tea, now letters, now an hour at the diary, now dinner – now, of course, a fight with Nellie, a scandal with Vanessa, but back to the desk and to critical writing. The days, rolling, one day after another like a great wheel. Doubt, too, coming round again and again to be resolved.

Something odd is happening with voice and time, I realize. I am trying to be linear where there is no linearity; it is repeat and repeat and repeat. Also, I am trying to contain. Trying to make sense of the surface of my relationship to Woolf and the impact and importance of her work to generations of women writers. I am squirming, as she did, to try and set the right tone – to not piss off the patriarchs, to hold the common reader in mind. I am also trying to do many things in one text, even though I know that part of how Woolf achieved the particular quality of clarity and wonder was having several projects in mind, if not on the go, at once; and those conversations can be heard across the books, echoing and filling each other in. She was writing AROOO on the heels of *Orlando*, for example, and so we see another perspective of the androgynous mind, and she was in the middle of essaying, and leaning from that into lectures, and thinking too of another way of saying all the same things, which we find in the beginnings of *The Waves*. In other words, all those works are present in the slim volume of AROOO, which we all carry like a literary bible in our bag.

When I begin to describe the project I am writing now to Jen Bervin, a familiar voice in my head rears up and asks, again, who I am to write this book? Who am I to respond to the great texts of other women writers at all, in particular *this* woman writer and *this* essential text? And now? Who are you to speak now? Now is not your moment. These sentiments live in my head, but I've also read them out in the world, sometimes referring to my previous books. I can anticipate the criticism: 'They need Woolf; Woolf does not need them.'

Woolf herself sometimes appears to inquire whether it is a pen or a pickaxe in my hand; though, despite her classism, I rarely feel that she would be embarrassed to have me identified with her, a kind of modern-day affliction where writers want to weed out and manage who is connected to their work, set out their own network of supporters, topped off with a kind of citational erasure. We are all looking at who our favourite writers cite. I prefer to be a conduit, a portal, a room people can move through. Woolf always affirms my decision.

On the other hand, when the young Ruth Gruber – the first to write a dissertation on Woolf's work – visited her in 1937, Woolf seemed not very encouraging and in fact barely registered Gruber's presence. And, according to S. P. Rosenbaum, of Woolf's visit to Newnham, the students who were in the room did not offer glowing reports and were offended by her description of their meals and academia itself; one student described Virginia and Vita sweeping in like rock stars – and who would not have wanted to witness that?

No, I thought, being self-sufficient is not necessarily being a lone or uncaring wolf. But also, we never know how readers are reading us, or audiences hearing us.

One of the great questions is, how do we show up for each other? How do we appreciate the writers we love? Also, how do we manage the relationship to our own room and the access of those we love to rooms of their own too? I have learned much from the millennials, and Gen Z, and Black women radicals about this; they have shone a light on where and what my generation lacked.

Now I pause with Lisa Robertson, looking out at the city – as though we are characters in Gail Scott's mind, 'indiscreetly spying on the writers' we were then, walking down Esplanade-by-the-Park so many years ago, in the Feminist City, writing our way to ourselves.

I am a flawed, working-class, queer writer, and also a flawed queer. I was never even gay in the right way. Always out of step. There's always someone who will dislike what you do, I tell myself, but few are as cruel to the self as the self can be.

I was relieved to be reminded of that, as I was walking along the edge of the city looking down at the Plateau. When considering the question, 'why Woolf?,' the answer that came to me is the same answer that always comes to me in these moments of clarity, in response to the question I ask myself constantly, which is, why do you return again and again to Woolf? *It is because the text made me!*

The text itself made me. It demanded a response. But it also literally *made me.*

And that is no small thing. Again and again, whenever I lose my way, I go back to Woolf. I go back to her texts and realign myself. Bring all the folds of my being into the work. I go back to the sentences that appear to contain whole trajectories – subtle and extensive – and look up into them. I feel a complicated lineage. They appear before me like cathedrals and street maps, like soft spaces to settle, like flares, sent up in moments of anguish and adoration, lighting a path I can always go down. They appear like furrows of joy I might harvest. They appear like girders, vertical and reeking of futures Woolf herself could not have foreseen.

One cannot write well unless one has dined well, slept well, and, I want to add – thinking of the way in which the women writers I admire describe their relationships, and how in the nineties we were all angry at Leonard – married well.

I can hardly imagine we would have had a Virginia Woolf in the canon had she married her good friend and one-time suitor, Lytton Strachey, to whom the artist Dora Carrington ended up serving as nursemaid. History is filled with ravaged couplings. There are very few literary unions that come out even-handed, concerned with mutual growth. Not that Strachey would have been menacing, but if Woolf's observations of his undermining behaviour, and the account of his life with Carrington, and Vita Sackville-West's dislike of the 'drooping Lytton,' are evidence, he would certainly have been self-absorbed. Woolf notes this herself in December 1929: 'Had I married Lytton I should never have written anything. So I thought at dinner the other night. He checks & inhibits in the most curious way. L. may be severe; but he stimulates. Anything is possible with him' (*Diary, Vol.* 3, 273).

Many women I know have had to escape violence in order to write. They have literally had to break out of relationships, to run for their lives. LGBTQ+ people are far more likely to experience violence. I have twice won an award for poetry named for Pat Lowther, the brilliant young West Coast poet and mother of two young girls who was murdered by her husband. I have written about Sylvia Plath, a poet who succumbed to her marriage. Elizabeth Smart had a clutch of children with the poet George Barker but never had him. Elizabeth Bishop had her Brazilian architect lover but her violence was alcohol, to which she sometimes succumbed.

In a letter to Vita, Virginia Woolf describes the American modernist poet Laura Riding in 1924, caught in a love triangle, who tipped her hat, said, 'So long, chaps,' and leapt out a window. In other words, the Beadle on the lawn – the figure that blocks Woolf's entrance to the library – very quickly becomes the Beadle in the bed beside us, and, then, the Beadle in our own minds.

The ramifications of these personal decisions are difficult to illustrate in creative writing workshops, but these choices are central to the question of 'how to have a writing life.' What one needs is so complicated, so varied, but there are strands, there are certain essential qualities. Partnership. Space. A door that locks. Community. Retreat. Consciousness.

Where do you want to be at the end of your degree, I ask my students. Mostly they have not thought of this at all. Even the graduate students. Even those who have a clear sense of themselves as writers aren't sure what that means for arranging their lives. I can't tell them, but I feel it's my job to create space for them to ask questions, to articulate what they want, and for me to affirm the reality of the working steps to create it. All is possible when you are aware of what is involved. The period after both of my degrees was demoralizing. I felt less prepared for life than I had at the outset.

Retreat, I saw early, is essential to writing, but dangerous to living. I ran into my beloved Prose professor on south Granville early in the fall of 1991, after completing my BFA from UBC. She asked how I was. Stunned, I might have said, disconsolate. But instead, I said, cheerfully, that I was great. And that I was looking for a cabin somewhere to go write. 'That's good,' she said, 'I think you are a writer, and you just have to go write.'

In late October of that same year, my good friend Berit, a Norwegian woman a decade older than I, whom I met waiting tables, took me to view a cabin on seven acres of rainforest at the edge of Qualicum Beach owned by Peter, an acquaintance of Berit, who lived, with her partner (also named Peter) above his workshop very near the small Qualicum Airport.

We wound our way up a long, narrow, curvy driveway that opened up onto a clearing which one felt, immediately upon stepping out of the car, lift one, like sails of air. To the left of where Berit parked there was an enormous barn. Big enough to build a boat, she pointed out, which Peter had done, and which he now sailed out of a harbour in Victoria – hence the empty property and need for stewards. Next to the barn sat a small, unadorned rectangular structure that housed a bathroom and a small room with two windows, nearly floor to ceiling, that looked out onto a pool of green.

Berit – one of the few women I had ever met who was taller than me – stood listening to the hum of the land (for it did feel as though the mossy earth below us was breathing) and the water making its way down through the trees. The birdsong lifted and sunk like bands of silk. The land had been logged, but that was long, long ago, and now the trees that towered over us seemed to be regarding our movements. There were crows overhead too, their metallic knock like bolts of energy, sharp and yet muffled, like someone lifting and shaking out the land. The clouds were a low grey ceiling, above which there were rumblings as if the upstairs neighbours were playing croquet.

We moved past the bathhouse along the length of the property, cleared in a figure eight, where a small, cedar-shingled chicken coop with a run was set, and then along the path behind that, which ended in a large, dark cedar grove, ringed with ferns. The path was overgrown there, or, it was a deer path that led to a garden I could see was enclosed by a waist-high chicken-wire fence made of lodge pole rails that would not be effective to keep out deer or anything other than a small dog.

We turned back, along the coop, then to the centre of the property, which had an overgrown garden on one side and on the other a rock so large it could have served as a patio with a table for two on top. Beyond that, a crudely made pond, surrounded by huckleberries, salal, and ferns. Then a wide, wide clearing, part of which was grass, and a second plateaued area that was cleared of trees, but not of shrubs, and high grasses, and beyond that a wall of forest with a hem like knots of thick black satin. There was a path through the centre of the back clearing that led, according to Berit, to a trail that cut through endless acres of Crown land.

I was beginning to think I had been mistaken that there was a cabin here at all, when across the grass I saw what appeared to be a tool shed at first glance, and a manger at second. The structure was built of cedar board and baton, long greyed, with a blue tarp-covered roof. There were a few flagstones marking an entrance, and a large, woody rhododendron filled with the ghosts of several seasons of dead blossoms. The structure itself appeared to be part of the forest that it backed onto.

I thought that calling this structure a cabin was lavish. The islands were filled with such structures built by draft dodgers and hippies. Inside the door there was a deep ceramic laundry sink with a rough-hewn countertop – more like a mudroom than a kitchen – but that was the only sink, and it had only one tap with cold water. In the main room there was a small old electric stove for cooking and a countertop the size of a cutting board. There was a small jag between walls with a shelf big enough for a teapot, and above that a forest portal at eye level. A kind of outdoor growing room could be accessed off the dining area that we would later seal off, along with half of the living room, to keep warm. The cabin seemed to have begun with this central dining area, then had the mudroom added, and another, bigger room where the woodstove sat. The bedroom had been added by cutting a hole near the woodstove. The structure was not safe, the roof wasn't more than a tarp over some boards; the floor, too, was boards over dirt. You could see through the cracks in the walls, and if you dropped a key or a pen on the floor it might fall through one of the spaces between the floorboards and never be retrieved. There was no bathroom, just an outhouse off in the forest – though there was a bathroom in the bathhouse near the barn.

Berit said that Peter had cut and milled each piece of wood himself; there was absolutely nothing even, nothing regular, polished, or precise to be seen anywhere. It would drive L., a carpenter of exacting lines, to distraction.

'I can imagine goats living in here,' I said, 'or bears.'

Peter had indeed come home one day to find a bear at the kitchen table eating what was left of breakfast. 'So,' Berit said, 'you are not far off. But think of what you could do!'

It was, I thought, unlivable. And, also, perfect.

I am never going to be dependent on another person ever again in my life! I meant this when I wrote it in my journal sitting in the Wembley Mall the day after seeing the cabin at Qualicum Beach. I had come over with L., and we were staying with her brother and sister-in-law in the house she and her work partner, Geoff, built for them on French Creek. I had a fantasy I would move in alone. For the moment, in any case, but I knew that L. had also been looking for a place – hopefully, Geoff, with whom she had been sharing a workshop, which they had just found out he would have to leave, and her old friend Andy, returned from a sojourn in Toronto. L. and Andy had lived together before I came along. Andy had the quality of a giraffe. You could hardly believe he moved at all, he was so slow and elegant, as if feeding only on the highest, ripest of fruit. He was mischievous, and expressed his gender in subtle, gentle ways, even as he was wielding a hammer, or helping L. lift up the side of a house. The three of them made for a surprising contracting crew: gentle, thoughtful misanthropists, mistrustful of all forms of governance, anti-capitalists with a keen awareness of climate collapse, impending dystopia, and social chaos. Together they would fall into discussions of moral imperatives: what to do to make change now? What was possible anymore? And how would we live in the fascisms of the future, for they were convinced they were coming.

I also had these fears, but I couldn't handle the intense negativity of their vision. What was the point, then, of even going off grid, as we'd dreamed? Of trying to create a small, alternative world? Here, I was confused. And, moreover, confused about collectivity, which I craved as much as solitude, dreaming utopias I didn't know how to realize.

By Christmas Eve we had moved into the cabin, having swept it out, sealed around the windows, and filled the cracks in the walls where we could. We also remade the bedroom. L. laid a new plywood floor; we painted it sage green, covered the freshly drywalled walls and ceiling with a coat of white, and trimmed the windows and floor with pine, before finally squeezing in a double bed that left little more than a foot on one side to crawl in and out of. When I swung open the window it hit a massive fir and the forest sounds washed into the room.

L.'s support of my desire to write was inconsistent. I felt it was commensurate with my own inconsistency. If I could only be more self-assured. More productive. More positive. Then she would be supportive in kind. I needed to earn the right to a room, not expect the room. It may not have been rational, but

I was disappointed when Geoff moved into the bathhouse that was to be my room – I was ashamed that I had had such a vision in the first place; it felt grand, beyond my worth. Room wasn't only a metaphor, it was more than a room; it was space, and space *in relation* to domesticity, not in it. It was a space that one had to encounter, a threshold one crossed to access, I thought, thinking of how Woolf crossed the space from Monk's House to her writing lodge, or descended into the bowels of 52 Tavistock Square. It was a space that built confidence.

As she notes in AROOO, one of the things men have is outer lives. They commute to work. They go elsewhere and return to the home to have their minds grounded but also held aloft in relation to the little fires of domesticity that burn at home. They are always able to see things in relation. To have pools of space outside of home. When I pressed about the bathhouse, L. was impatient.

I had nothing against Geoff, who was good company – close to family – although L. had not disclosed to him that she was a lesbian or acknowledged us as a couple.

'Obviously, I knew,' he said, years later when I returned to pick up the last of my things, 'but she never acknowledged it to me. Not once.'

Which is impressive, I thought. L. was a person who stuck close to what worked for her. 'You have to go for what you want,' she had told me early on in our relationship. 'Otherwise, I'll mow you down. Not intentionally, but because I will fight for what I want with everything I have.' And she did fight. She achieved a brown belt in Karate, she took up racquetball and won tournaments; whatever she did, she did to win, and I admired her work ethic. She was all about bootstrap, which I also identified with. Almost from the moment our relationship began, she had expressed a desire for personal rather than communal success.

It was the combination of her self-discipline and commitment to community that I was attracted to, even as my own deep interiority and lack of social skills made it difficult for me to feel part of any community. I liked my status, not as 'coach's wife,' a phrase I had heard used to describe me, but as co-creator of something new.

So what to do about the room? The 'almost enoughness' of our relationship was painful. We could see in each other the right qualities, but not in the right context, or the right moment, and leaving the extended network of lesbians in the city was not helpful. Suddenly we were faced with the intolerance of small-town life, something which I knew about, having grown up in many of them and found myself beaten up on several occasions for being queer.

She had forgotten the struggle she had undergone coming out into a world of extremely closeted, very heterosexually shaped couples who adhered to strict butch–femme codes. She had come up through that scene to create a world of more loosely defined sexual relationships, co-ops, queer artists, lesbian soccer teams – she had gone from player to coach. Now we were in a community where there were no out queers around us – not that we had seen yet, in any case, though we would come to know the lesbian community in Errington, and then through my doctor in Nanaimo the lesbian community there and on Gabriola. So, too, our friend Greg, battling AIDS, would come home to spend time with his family in Lantzville and take the poetry workshop I would later audit. But all of our queerness – his, mine, L.'s – would be pushed to the margins.

When one of the two sisters-in-law that lived within a stone's throw from our property gave all the siblings except L. the gift of a family portrait at a studio for the holidays that year, I was incensed on her behalf and humiliated for myself. When asked why, the sister-in-law laughed as if L. was insane: 'Why on earth would you want a family portrait? You don't have a family.'

The white velvet cabbage moths of summer circled overhead in pairs, high over the trampoline where joy erupted, and where sometimes, in the height of the summer star season, I slept. We had all settled into life in the hollow, as I referred to it. The garden was filled with toppling sunflowers. My sister France had come and created windchimes of shells she gathered from Rathtrevor. L. set up an outdoor kitchen with a tarp over it and we assembled a long table made of a panel of glass found at a job site, ringed with an assortment of found chairs so that the whole thing resembled the table Snoopy lays out for Charlie Brown's Thanksgiving dinner.

Where L. and I met was in our love of the land. When nothing else was working we had that. She drove around on a battered moped, rake in hand, clearing sticks so guests could set up tents and we could play badminton or croquet. I some-times napped in the afternoon with the window open against the fir and could hear the forest sounds so distinctly – I was once awoken by the snap of a spider cracking a beetle in half. Sometimes, I napped on the trampoline L. and Geoff had bought. Looking up, it felt like we were in the bowl of a moun-tain range. I traced the peaks as I lay there. Sometimes L. lay beside me and we counted satellites. Sometimes there was a bonfire and much laughter. She was the kind of person, silent and affable, who attracted very loyal, fun friends. If they only knew what was going on inside my mind, she said once. What do you mean, I asked. Nothing, she said, there's zero going on in there, but if you remain silent people think you're wise. But you are wise, I said. Really? It was a rare moment of doubt for her. But I knew, whatever our situation might be, that it was true. She was wise. And good.

The moths flitted high over the hammock hanging between two fir trees so thick I couldn't wrap my arms around either of them. I was into soundtracks that summer and had bought those to *A Room With a View* and *The Mission*, and I lay reading in the temperate rainforest with its gentle, gentle summer breeze. Woolf, yes, but not only. Strewn about on the grass was always a mix of literature – *Best American Fiction*, popular novels by Amy Tan, Maxine Hong Kingston, Jamaica Kincaid, Barbara Kingsolver, and a friend had sent Elizabeth Smart's *The Assumption of Rogues and Rascals*.

My prized possession was the complete softcover set of Woolf's diaries, which L. had bought me from a used bookshop in LA. Prior to this I had carried around the condensed version – *A Writer's Diary* – which was instruction enough. Now I had the whole of it. Points on a literary life from beginning to end. I had taken to reading them every morning – as the seasons changed – and copying sentences. They filled me with such joy; like suddenly knowing how to do a backflip, I could leap across the page.

My mind was thick and slow with the noise of the hollow; the chickens floated across the grass like rogue handmaidens, bloomers bunched at their sides; Thelma, the black cat, dozed in her basket on the roof, where she hunted for mice at night, dropping them at the foot of the door below her before curling back into her bed. My own cat, Sadie, whom I had brought home from a loft party on Main Street in Vancouver years before, had a red collar with a bell to warn the birds she hunted at the pond. She would seem, by the end of our time there, to have become feral, looking more like a raccoon than a cat. When I went for a walk with the dogs, she would sometimes follow us far into the woods, traceable only by the occasional tinkle of her bell or a glimpse of her slinking through the thick underbrush.

Now the *knock, knock* of the red-headed woodpecker, the sudden shadow and tear of crow, the buzz of bees in the garden and the hummingbirds at the feeders that L. hung like drops of amethyst from the beam of the woodshed.

Now the mad rogue chicken charged across the grass to snatch up a mouse Sadie was hunting, tossing it high in the air and swallowing it in one dramatic gulp.

Sweet domes of heat gathered, still innocent then, in the last decade of the twentieth century, as I dozed in the hollow. I wanted, as I had found in *The Waves*, total immersion. I dreamed of being part of the garden. And I was. What was less certain was my relationship.

In retrospect, I still have no idea what changed. There was an increase in incidences of impatience. I noticed people wince now and then after something she said to me. I didn't like the feeling of dependence, which she kept urging. On the one hand, don't bother working, on the other hand, 'I can't live with someone who doesn't wake up in the morning with joy … ' She did wake very early, filling the wood stove, making coffee, and heading out with Geoff to whatever job they were in the middle of. I woke up hours later in a fog in the overheated room.

I set up a tent where I could sleep. 'Maybe we could build a writing room,' I tried one day. 'Could we make it so that it could be moved? So that it could be taken apart?'

'Why do you need someplace special to *not write* anyhow? Don't you think you'd have published something by now if you were meant to do that?'

I felt my legs buckle under me. Yes, I thought, wouldn't I have?

'L.,' Andy said, raising his eyebrows at her.

'I'm just kidding,' she said. 'But does anyone write anything of value before they're thirty?'

Sometime that summer, Andy left to build a cabin with a mutual friend, one with deeper roots than he and L.

I worked nights with Berit at the restaurant where we often stayed after our shifts to complain about our relationships. Otherwise, I read, tried to write. What was I writing? The start of a play here, story there, poem there. Nothing was coming together. I was so uneven, spending huge amounts of energy making jam, or puttering in the garden, then spiralling into a depression where I could not see myself finding a way to balance all the tasks. Then doing nothing.

Then came Woolf scholars and critics Louise DeSalvo and Roger Poole. I read both that summer: Poole's depiction of Woolf as being oppressed and harassed by Leonard was disturbing, but not as disturbing as DeSalvo's portrayal of Woolf as an incest survivor. I'm not sure what came first that summer, recurring images of myself in my brother's bed, or the scenes of Woolf and her brother Gerald Duckworth that Louise DeSalvo makes so vivid in her book on Woolf and her childhood sexual abuse – add to that the news, that summer, of Woody Allen and his step-daughter Soon-Yi, and the ongoing discussion of who to believe, I walked around feeling nauseated and I could not shake the sensation of being held down, or submerged under water. I take DeSalvo's book down from my shelf to try and trace those scenes, but even now, decades later, I find those sentences triggering.

It was depressing to be right back where I'd started, before the long battle of the undergraduate degree, in my mind, and work. I was better read, with some clearer sense of what I wanted out of writing, but with no idea how to proceed, and with no clearer sense of how to find myself equally in my relationship, which had now begun to pain me.

I didn't want to sleep in the same bed with L. anymore, and I felt it was my fault. It was my failure to keep the strands of my past at bay.

Woolf's early life at Hyde Park Gate, the 'little backwater' as her father describes it, is affluent and yet not 'as' affluent as others (the way wealth and privilege carry on). The Stephen family had no carriage, for example, and her mother went out on her rounds (aiding the ill and impoverished) on the bus, sitting next to the driver if possible and taking in all of his stories, which were then relayed to the rest of the household while she filled teacups around the great round table on the first of six floors.

Woolf moves from room to room, from world to world, always aware of the membrane between herself and others – like living inside a grape – the protective coating that preserves the innermost self from the constant shaping of hands, always hands, on young bodies

Stuck. As Elizabeth Bowen reflects, no one who accomplished what she did was ever still.

Here, like a cat, the Woolf I love steps right into my lap, shifting herself and licking her fur as she circles around and around, trying to unsettle Gerald Duckworth's imprint on her being. Here, the full weight of her empathy blooms, rising and filling not only my lap but the room I am in, lush and full of textures, it laps from wall to wall to wall. But also, here she taps into the marrow of sorrow; never fear sorrow, never pull back, enter it just as you enter a lake in August. She pillories me so sweetly I upend and float through the caught house of my own childhood, out the door, down the hall. That is what we want, freedom from the trapped rooms of our childhood. Years and years I spent navigating these rooms. Up to the attic where my young body would be caught on a cross-beam, or down, down I would sink so deep into the basement where the ghosts were: the settlers of the Red River, the First Nations who gathered by the banks, the bones and fragments of theft, desire, colonialism. What was the distance between the colonial mind and the mind of a man who could lift a child onto a mantle in a hallway? There was something repugnant at the essence of male sexuality. Vita Sackville-West writes to her husband of Virginia's deep hatred and mistrust of it.

I can go back to that corner of my childhood either in my mind or in the material world, or via Google Street View, and virtually nothing has changed: not the house, nor the neighbouring houses on either side, nor the apartment building across the street, nor the school, nor the boat club on the riverbank, nor my sense of being trapped in those rooms. I could feel anger in the bones of the dead at the riverbank, a yearning to move beyond the acceptance of the narrow margins of gender, and of our way of deciding what another body can or cannot do, one body deciding that it can use other bodies, as randomly and casually as fuel, as pleasure, as labour, as tools.

Long before Virginia Woolf's Orlando wandered his estate longing to write, a young Virginia Stephen moved through the house she grew up in, from the upper floors of her father's library down to the salon where her half-brother, George Duckworth, paced, setting plans for his rise through the social classes of London – longing to write. The house was divided, she writes, in 'A Sketch of the Past'; there were two worlds, the socially minded society-climbing world of the Duckworth brothers and the intellectual world of her father at work in his library above. Her father, whom she casts as the oppressive intellectual rock, the grinding presence who will die of cancer in 1904 after an iconic literary life. The kind of drawing-room literary maleness who memorized poems to recite after dinner. Moreover, to hear echoes of Woolf herself sprung from those lines. Like the men she describes in Chapter Two of *AROOO*, Virginia Woolf herself had more mobility than most young women. Education inequalities aside – not making light of them, but shifting them away for a moment – she could move back and forth from one floor, one room, to another – already rich in perspective, able to see herself outside of herself and in relation to the worlds she moved through. Triangulating her way *out* of the small rooms of her youth.

There is nothing, in my mind, more painful than losing a child, except maybe the children around the lost child, the children experiencing death too early, but even worse is the aftermath, which is so often loneliness. I recently heard trauma described as being left alone with one's pain.

I did not want to think of Woolf as having been permanently scarred because Gerald Duckworth lifted her onto the shelf by the mirror at Hyde Park Gate and fondled her. This scene dovetails completely and unfortunately with my own experience of childhood. Several moments that had solidified to the point they were immovable in the centre of my mind, like the small tumour that had nestled there.

It wasn't a shelf, but the bed in my brother's room where he lifted me and not only fondled me but convinced me to touch him, which was, in a way, worse because it made me have some kind of agency; and then the window at the bottom of the staircase that caught my reflection as I tried to climb down to my mother's room for comfort; and then a while later, staring down the same set of stairs to see the policemen arriving with news of my brother's fatal accident, and my mother fainting, and then the endless guilt and shame of his hands on me, a bond that would never loosen, never dissolve.

The other sensation, too, is the disconnect of joy carrying on around me outside the room. Nostalgia is a drug, it's true. It's the opium of the abused child. The noise of family life carrying on outside the bedroom door still haunts. It instilled in me the hard muscle of narrating things to make sense, making them blend into the larger narrative of family life as we are supposed to experience it. It's a sensation woven into the fabric of my being that I will never undo, that I will always and forever fall prey to. The moment is caught. It's a weight the body wears that shifts slightly, but like a ring of external feelings, like the rings of Saturn.

☥

'You're laughable,' L. said. She had come home mid-morning and caught me mumbling at the kitchen table. When I tried to explain what was happening in my mind and my body, she sighed.

'Why do you think your pain is any more vivid or important than anyone else's?'

'I don't think that. It's just what I have to deal with.'

'You'll never have anything positive to say about pain. You like to wallow in it.

I flushed with rage, yelling as she left that I was going to get a new lock and she should not bother to come back, then slamming the door after her. I had a burst of confidence in that moment, but before I made my way the ten or so steps back to the kitchen table, she had already come in through the bedroom window. She was strong and in possession of a brown belt in martial arts and she easily flipped me onto the floor with a thud, grabbing my collar and pulling my face close to hers: 'Don't you ever close a door on me. Not ever. Do you understand?'

I could hear L. chuckling as she walked away from me. I had in me two minds. Two bodies. The one I was in, and the one observing the one I was in and the one that I could see beyond where L.'s head had been looking down at me. Leaving heterosexuality had not saved me from this, I thought. Why had I thought being in a lesbian relationship would be any different? I had seen the fights. The butches dragging their women out of the bar, just like the fights in the bar at the Terrace Hotel where I had worked as a teenager. Bodies flying across tables on Saturday night, and when the first affair I'd had, with the drummer in a touring all-girl band at the hotel where my sixteen-year-old body worked, was discovered by her partner, a golden-throated Mexican-American woman from California whose mother worked her entire life in a Campbell's soup factory, followed me into the bathroom and smashed my head against the metal divider multiple times before heading off to find the drummer and do the same thing to her. Violence, alcohol, and coke were my introduction to queer life. Leather-clad bodies piled on hotel-room beds. A kind of bravado I followed for several years, down a trail of burned-out hotel rooms and near rapes, before settling down with L. I had a lot to thank her for. I knew that. And yet I did not feel safe.

I revisit the pages of my journal from that summer, and beside me, Woolf's 'A Sketch of the Past,' which I had open on the kitchen table that day, with my tea. I could see it from the floor, where I lay for a long time wondering what I had gotten myself into. And wondering how I was going to get out.

What was love anyhow? Maybe, I thought, I had no idea.

Chapter Five

How was it that Woolf could keep so many strands alive, and in control? How, with all this rambling and circularity, and falling into despair, was I to find a way forward? I walked in the salal, far out into the woods with the dogs; I walked from the cabin to the bathhouse, to the chicken coop to collect eggs, and to my garden to pick peas and pluck carrots that I ate warm in the sun. The deer sheared the long lines of bean leaves, but they did not eat the beans themselves. So too the small garden snakes disturbed nothing about the potatoes as they curled up to sleep.

The sounds of the hollow, the stretch of air when I opened the cabin door, all felt like part of my body and a thing I pushed ahead of me like a cart. It was languorous, erotic, and outside. Still, now that I could hear the most minute disturbance of air, I would never want to miss any of it – not the robin song, nor the crow, not the warblers nor the white-throated sparrow. When I moved, I moved with and in their song. The crows tugged me toward the cedar grove, where the deer slept; the chickadees tumbled headlong down the fir.

But the sentences did not spread out like the knock of a beak. How did Woolf do it? How did she transfer the body to the page, capture the air and the sounds? I asked again and again, picking up my tattered copies of *The Waves*, *Orlando*, and *A Room of One's Own* – how did she organize her life? What came first? How was time stacked?

I knew that I needed to extend control of my craft, but so much of what I had to focus on was mechanics. The writing needed to be second nature. I had to gear up to a pace at which I could fly, not encumbered by the parts of a sentence, which, if you had asked me at this time, I could not have named. I would not learn them until I started teaching Expository Writing at Rutgers University in New Jersey a decade later. It was going to take several lifetimes to reach the state of equanimity and interconnectedness that Woolf had found in her lifetime. I knew that it was an unachievable goal, and here I wasn't thinking of the genius of her texts but, rather, the genius of her living. Making the best possible world for that to come to fruition for myself – that was my goal. My own potential. That was what I was chasing. And for that, I would need a voice.

Meanwhile, I had found that there was an organization dedicated to the study of Woolf. Incredulous, I sent a note and received, to my surprise, some weeks later in the mail, an invitation to join the society, signed by a young scholar named Mark Hussey.

On the other hand, L. was right. Wasn't she? I should have come, if not to publication, then to a sense of being a part of the contemporary world of writing, among my peers, in conversation by now. Was there really nothing I could say? I couldn't shake the desire for my room, which I saw always, out of the corner of my eye, perched at the edge of the forest, in a pool of calm. Distraction, distraction, I told myself and set my hands to manual labour.

One day, in frustration, I dropped my gardening tools, wiped my hands, got into my little blue Fox and left the hollow, driving down to Nanaimo, to my old poetry professor's office at Malaspina. He was there, Professor Smith, now simply Ron, sorting through one of the many shelves of poetry books. He was also a publisher of poetry, and I rarely left his office without a new book. I told him what was happening: not about the failure of my relationship, and how unsafe I felt, but with my work, or lack of forward momentum. None of this, he assured me, was out of the ordinary. Writing lives were long, they took time to get established, take root. I knew this from his workshop: dedication to craft was everything; poems couldn't be rushed. But what is the best way to earn a living while writing, I finally asked. How am I to earn my 500 pounds?

'Ah,' he said, sitting back and putting his fingers together in front of him like a little cathedral. 'Pat and I assumed you were independently wealthy. You always seem to have everything under control.'

This was the problem, I thought. The appearance of ease I gave. I was generally too proud to show my accounts, usually at zero, or less than. I had little money of my own. None, really. The life I dreamed of was enmeshed with L., who was both supportive of and frustrated by my situation. How much better was it to be dependent on a woman than a man? None, as far as I could see. Dependent is dependent.

I wandered around the library where I had spent my first successful year of post-secondary education reshelving books and reading as I went. Professor Norton's librarian mother was at her station. She looked small. Frail. The library, too, seemed to have shrunk. Now, after the libraries at UVic and UBC, the poetry section here felt so familiar. I had been overwhelmed when I first started working there, thinking I would never make it through all the books. I wouldn't, of course, but I was a little less panicked about it now, having swum in larger stacks.

What was holding me back? Was it the 500 pounds? Was it a lack of craft? Story? A style of my own? Lack of discipline? Credit card debt was constant. But even if I had found money, what good would it be if hands could reach up out of the depths of my psyche and press my head down so that I sometimes felt I had to struggle for air? How was I going to move on from that?

I left the library empty-handed and headed back to the car, but with every step I seemed to be less clear about who I was. Not the usual existential question, but the basic contact with the moment. I had the sensation that I had slipped out of my body. I closed my eyes a minute, thinking that if I opened them, I would see myself floating away over the parking lot toward the Georgia Strait. This floating above myself often happened at night in my childhood beds, and sometimes so visceral was the sensation that I had been flying I would wake up and have motion sickness. Turning now, there was nothing, or no one. I touched my arm – yes, it was my arm. I slowed as if I were being followed. Great swishes of energy, as if I were tied to a mast, seemed to be trailing me. And then I felt like I was back inside the bell jar. Sounds dimmed. I looked ahead and suddenly I had no idea where I was. Or who I was. I looked at the car I was standing next to. It was mine; I was certain of that. But did I want to drive? I looked out across Nanaimo to the sea and thought that it would be good to be inside *that*. The sea, that is. I slid into the seat. I put the key into the ignition. I would find a road – possibly near Cedar, I thought, near the petroglyphs, not the ferry – a road with a boat launch at the end. I would drive into the sea.

The world was, and was not, the same. I recognized the materiality of the place, a cross between a small town and suburb, with a bare lot here and there, trees, trucks, cars, bicycles. Tiny flickers of panic seemed to lack the force to penetrate my body. There was a larger calmness that was equally eerie. *Just breathe*, I thought, *and get to the sea*. There was another voice too, though, a quiet, insistent voice telling me that some-thing was not right. Something was not right at all. I heard it, but I kept driving. Floating really. So slowly that cars honked and passed me with waves of aggression. Then I heard a voice saying *Turn here!* And I did. I found myself on the main street in Nanaimo, but I might as well have been on the moon. I saw a parking spot and slid into it. I had to get out of the car, I realized, because I had no idea what I was doing. I walked very slowly down the street, stunned. Then there were hands on my shoulders, from behind.

'Hello?'

'Hello,' I said. I couldn't see who it was.

'Can I help you?'

'I don't know, can you?'

'Where are you going? What are you looking for?'

'I don't know,' I replied, and then, to my own surprise, from the depths of my unconscious came a name someone, at some point, must have offered me.

The hands lifted.

I stood at a traffic light for several runs through. Now the cars stopped. Now they jerked forward. I could hear the gears, I thought, and the way the rubber held the road like a thousand tiny locks, and below that a kind of incessant drone of rage. There were many voices too, on the street, and they flowed around me like water around a rock.

Then a jolt. I opened my eyes. Closed them. Hands on my shoulder again. Opened my eyes. Nanaimo, 1992.

'Over there,' a voice said. Then she – it sounded like a she – pushed me a little and I started crossing the street. 'You're nearly there, just a few doors down,' another push. Gentle. Another push. 'There's a red door, you go in and up the stairs; the person you want is the first door on the left.'

I turned to say thank you, but whoever it was had vanished.

I climbed the stairs and knocked on the door and it opened. Once I saw her face, I understood that this was the therapist my doctor had spoken to me about, and all the flimsiness of the world diminished. She didn't seem at all surprised to see me. Could I come the following Tuesday? Yes, I said. Was I able to get home? Yes, I said.

I was deeply exhausted and wished only to sleep.

In photos of myself at that time I often have a gaunt look, as my mother often did, too thin and in clothes that were too big, a bit cheap, frayed, misaligned. Ravaged, as Marguerite Duras described herself in *The Lover*. Caught in a loop of reliving and retelling the same story. The one story. The man who arrives to pick up her young body and ravish it again and again. How, I thought, thinking of Ron and his wife assuming I had it all together – how was this looking like I had it all together?

I don't believe my disarray was as romantic as Duras' or Jean Rhys', or Woolf's for that matter, muttering in her bath and scaring the servants. But I took solace in it. In my twenties, I often had to take to bed with migraines. I would forget to eat and fade off into what I realized a few years later were hypoglycemic episodes; I might forget to get off the bus, or drive past my turnoff. In my journal, the dates are wrong so often. I barely know what year it is. I was so thin my pants buckled around the belt. I leaned in. I looked down. I always looked down.

I spent the first session with Moira, who I later found out went by Hawk Owl, in silence.

The room was very busy, filled with talismans and masks, bits of feather and a bowl, fabrics and textures; something like a kimono hung on the wall. A musky cedar smell hung in the air. I felt grateful for the space, but I was not at ease in it. Not at all. And, worse, I could sense her impatience, so I wanted to perform what was expected of me.

I had not told L. of the incident in the parking lot, or how I got to the therapist – and I did not know how I was going to pay for it either, for that matter, but she had said there was a sliding scale.

In the silence I closed my eyes and let my mind sink and sink until I felt I was down a well.

I was about to fall asleep when Hawk Owl got up and came over to me.

She was quite a big woman, with the clunky jewellery professors of a certain era all seemed to wear, so much so that her face becomes superimposed with the director of women's studies from my time at UVic, and with the women's studies professor at Malaspina.

'Are you going to speak?'

I didn't move. She put her hand on the back of my head. 'Are you going to react?' I didn't move. After a few minutes she pushed my head down to my knees. 'Are you going to react now?' I didn't move. Down further, to my ankles. I didn't move. Then down until my head was on the floor. 'Are you ever going to react?'

'No,' I said finally, breaking my own silence.

Dr. Winder, my new lesbian doctor – I can't recall how she came to me – had given me several gifts over that summer without my asking: a mysterious remedy for what she described as my stuckness (I feel I should warn L., she said, but I will resist the urge), Moira's name – which slipped into my consciousness, then rose to the surface at the right moment – and finally, a connection that led to my being able to live, temporarily, in a small house of my own that clung to a rocky outcrop in Nanoose Bay. It was furnished with a sofa and a table, which was almost all that could fit. I used the kitchen table as a desk, which I set by the front window, next to a bed that Geoff made out of rough two-by-fours. From where I sat I looked out over the ocean framed by arbutus trees, where seals popped up and winds lashed at the glass as I slept.

As much as I had loved the hollow, and the cabin with its ghostly plastic cutting the living room in half, I knew I had to leave L. She had initially been angry that I left, but very soon after began to come and do her laundry – I had always done our laundry, in the laundromat in Qualicum Beach, walking near the water as I waited to shift it from washer to dryer – and to have dinner and sometimes sleep, so tight in the little bed that we couldn't shift our bodies. She brought gifts of firewood for the stove. I couldn't afford to order a cord of wood on my own and had to content myself with buying packages from the gas station on the highway with tip money from yet another restaurant job I had found, this time in Nanaimo.

When the storms came, it felt like I was clinging to a raft in a washing machine. It was turbulent. Loud. I was so surprised when, in the morning, the arbutus was still there, knuckles on rock, and the sky cleared. I woke early because windows, windows, windows; sometimes there was water on the inside of the sliding glass doors.

The woman who owned the larger house to which this cabin was a guest house was widowed and a patient of my doctor. She spent her days walking her dog, making meals, watching TV. I was so envious of her wealth, the expanse of space, several floors of windows overlooking the water. She had a white bull terrier and they walked like two strokes of white paint against the sky. I never saw her eyes. Only the back of her head entering the house, and leaving.

I was envious not only of her house on the water, but of all the time she seemed to have on her hands, and moreover, how calm she was in it. I was here, but it was a band-aid solution. I was never going to be able to afford to stay. The postal carrier told me there were at least a half-dozen screen and TV writers in this postal code. He had noticed the studio addresses.

'Who would I be if I wasn't always searching for a way to make money?' I said out loud one day.

'You don't have to search for money,' L. reiterated. 'You don't need money. You only have to accept your life.'

It was my ongoing failure, I thought, that I couldn't find a way to simply be her wife.

Something – the room of my own, Ron's workshop, which I had begun to audit, the passing of time, my reading, or else Dr. Winder's remedy, or all of it at once – did its work. In the fall of 1992, the words began to come, sporadically, but with energy, textures, and surprising images; they were rhythmic, with fresh associations and movement, attuned to something beyond the usual for me, and yet more relational and intuitive than anything I had ever produced.

If I closed my eyes, I could feel the energy, the hum at the centre of the work I so desired to do. It reminded me of my first encounter with Woolf, with *The Waves*. Now I was here again, but the waves, this time, I could see were all elegy; they were filled with childhood, bubbling, innocent, and brutal, the harsh lines insistent, repetitive as morning. It was here, the points connecting and the line staying free. I had only, I thought, to get out of my own way. Let a logic assemble before me. But how? How was I doing that on the page? And could I do it, too, in life?

I stayed with my thoughts, I stayed with the work, and language began to accumulate in my mind when I walked with my dog, and when the rhythm hit, the poems seemed to pour onto the page with an ease that shook me. I started printing them out with the elegant Mac StyleWriter I had bought during my last months at UBC and tacking them to the long bare wall of my cabin. They looked like garden plots on the page: square, square, rectangle, and in those shapes, textures curving up, up, up, now like great fields of lavender, now like canola, now like corn, now like a forest, now light spreading across the page.

I brought them into the workshop I was auditing at Malaspina with Professor Smith.

'These are really good,' Ron said. 'And they seem to come easily to you. You should do a bunch and send them out, you should "knock off a hundred," and make a book. Then,' he said, after a beat, 'You should go to grad school and then come back here and take my job.'

Easily was a gross oversimplification, I thought, feeling the weight of the empty months, but it was true, they seemed to be pouring out of me. Still, they were poems. And it was prose I was after, even if it was poetry that seemed most natural and poets the most welcoming. I sent a few poems out to the journal I had heard about while at UVic – the one Constance Rooke edited – and later, in the winter, I would receive notice of their acceptance.

I then applied to grad school. Only to one. Concordia, in Montreal. I had no idea what it meant to go to grad school, or how to approach applications, but I knew I had to move forward. I knew that grades mattered, and, looking at my transcript, I realized that the French class I didn't complete, and the American literature class I finished under protest, had both earned me only passing grades, and that these Ps had dragged my otherwise solid GPA down to a second class, which meant that there were few options for graduate school.

My dreams for nearly thirty years were rooted in the room of my five-year-old self. I never went far from it, even if I got out (in reality, the room itself was short-lived) in life, or sometimes in the dreams, flying out of a window just as it ignited into flames, or shooting out through a crack in the wall down the hallway, up, up like a helium balloon to the top of the house where I bumped and floated in the ribs of the roof; there was no real escape.

Invariably I would be back in that room the next night, and the next, in the bed where I had no place to hide, in the room that could change shape around me: now a classroom, now a cave somewhere, maybe on the Red River, or on the moon – it was always the same feeling in the room. The cave could contain a whole universe of children being handed off to men who entered the room and exited. This happened because of exhaustion. Mother figures too depleted to think.

This memory comes back with ferocity as I walk through Mile End in late summer of 2021 with a former student, discussing the possibility of grad school. She has arrived a little late, in a fog herself after a difficult night of dreams, she says.

'He's always there, chasing me. There is no way out.'

'Ah,' I say, 'I think I know that dream.'

'Does it ever end?'

'Not without intentionality,' I say. 'This is what I spent the second year of my graduate degree doing: learning to get out of that room. To do that I had to learn how to enter my own dreams, so that I could change the outcome.'

It isn't until I say this out loud that I realize this is one thing I am trying to make clear in this book. The way that there can seem to be no exit at all from the trauma of the body. That it is ongoing. That we have all accepted this, not only for us, but for our children. And for our students. And that the room can be a place that keeps us apart from ourselves and the world. The room can easily become a closed door. A locked place. A prison of our own devising, or our own resignation, and that we have to get out.

Since it is located in the centre of the country – Winnipeg, the place all the railway lines must pass through – and I have lived either on the West Coast or in the East, visiting the original house where the room is, the material location of my long nightmare, requires a lot of effort.

To my knowledge, none of my other siblings has ever bothered to go back to visit the house we inhabited the night our eldest brother passed away, though I know that each of their lives were altered by his death, this brother who molested me, and also molested my two sisters, and who knows about my other two brothers? As far as I know, none of them had any interest in this house or in the grave where our brother is buried, or the city where some part of our childhood exists still. For me, it is there, but it is also a rock in the throat that every speech act must navigate. A boulder in the middle of my mind all my thinking must press against. A linguistic block that will not allow my father tongue to live in me.

It is an altar. It calls and calls.

A molested child thinks they are hiding their wounds but they blink like neon all over, sending out signals, it seems, that attract ever more of the same.

I have carried my father's ashes to scatter on this brother's grave, and then my mother's ashes. Each time I visit his grave I drive by the room, and each time I visit the room I drive by the grave. I drive to the street, which has not changed in thirty years, and to the house, which has changed only modestly, and I stand under the window calling for myself.

In 1994 I had the fortune of finding a room under the room of the woman I would spend the rest of my life with, even marry, after seventeen years together. I had largely avoided her over the course of the first year of grad school because I knew I had a crush, but upon my return to the squalid room of my good friend with whom I was to stay, I found the situation untenable and so I called her – we had only landlines then – and she answered in a fog saying she had a migraine and couldn't speak.

I knew migraines well and so went over with Advil and a plant. She opened the door, her green eyes glinting out from a mane of curls, took the items, and receded. I didn't know if I would ever see her again, but a few days later she phoned and invited me for dinner. The room below her, she said, hearing about my situation, was unoccupied. She gave me the name of the landlady and, soon after, I moved in.

It was in this room that I spent the most focused weeks on my dreams: methodically working myself up to sleep every night.

I had been locked in these dreams as long as I could remember, possibly even before my brother passed away, but since my time in the hollow, they had taken on extra-disturbing dimensions, and I felt myself falling into them on the street, or in class, where it felt like I was frozen. This also took the form of panic attacks, which had escalated so intensely that once while on the ferry from Horseshoe Bay to Nanaimo I tried to convince the captain to turn the boat around because I was convinced I would die if I reached the other side.

The original figure with the knife in my dream was, I believe, a neighbour, but it could easily have been the brother who molested me. I assume that he was also molested. I see his face in his altar-boy outfit standing next to a priest and it sets my teeth on edge. I assume my own father, too, as I recall his stories of the priests in the small church at Saint-Crépin, and then later at the boarding school he attended in Aix-en-Provence. Where does any story really begin?

Whoever it was, this figure in my dreams with the knife, coming for me in my bed, he is eerily enmeshed with the 1967 hit 'Windy.'

My time in the hollow had been, I realized only later, a slow crisis of connecting with the trauma of those years. Reading Louise DeSalvo was the height of the nightmare. I didn't want Woolf's talent reduced to a creative response to childhood molestation as much as I didn't want Evelyn Lau to be reduced to the experiences she wrote about in *Runaway*, or Dorothy Allison her character in *Bastard Out of Carolina*, which I had recently read. Perhaps all my desire to write could be explained away as 'having been molested.' This is something that happened to women, the molesting part, and then the 'explaining away' part. Worse, there was, in tandem with discussion about childhood sexual abuse, a rise in claims of False Memory Syndrome, which accused therapists of drawing out certain strands in narratives. That, and the repeated description of certain books (Allison's *Bastard Out of Carolina*, for instance) as humourless, victim-centred narratives, made me extremely uneasy about how to navigate my own story.

That fall, miles and miles away from the hollow, and L., in my basement room, my dreams intensified and sprawled: there was plenty of the ongoing dream of the rapist, but there were also new variations with a kind of playfulness that startled me. I remember one in which, when the nightmare achieved appropriately sexual proportions, I found myself trapped in a building made entirely of rooms that were replicas of my childhood room, each with a more perverse dominatrix at the helm, ready to whip me into some kind of pleasurable submission. In another, I found my way to the attic window (for sure a deviation from being trapped inside), but now I was faced with the inevitable question one faces in dreams such as these – do I try to jump or wait to be caught again? – when a giant, beautifully shaped aubergine (a vegetable I associated very closely with my love object) appeared dangling from a crane above my head.

But that wasn't the final dream.

How her mind burned, I thought, opening *AROOO* to a random page as I sorted through the few books I brought with me to Montreal. How it burned, a pure, clear flame. I pulled out my set of Woolf's diaries and novels and set my course. Woolf was like the prow of a ship, cutting through the literary world around her, sorting new books into piles of interesting and dull. She burned and plowed, condensing whole afternoons down to half a line: 'Thirty-seven people to tea; a bunch of young men no bigger than asparagus; walking to & fro, round & round … ' (*Diary, Vol. 2*, 243).

The tone of her wit was the right tone. Even when it was cutting. The slice was always just right, the burning just the right heat: it never succumbed to anger and bitterness, though sometimes, I realized – and I was relieved to find Elizabeth Hardwick had also noticed – she was mean. She bared her teeth around class. The way that the tutor, Miss Kilman, in *Mrs. Dalloway* is described as 'the object of the author's insolent loathing.' No, Hardwick notes, 'Miss Kilman is not evil, she is merely unappetizing. Her social and personal defects are confronted in a peculiarly exasperated mood, without pity or inhibition.' As if there were something sentimental about poverty itself. 'The poor don't understand humour,' Woolf lamented, when she was asked to join the Rodmell branch of the Women's Institute in November 1940.

How her mind burned, I could have also said about the woman who lived in the room above me, whom I would walk to school with, and whom I would eventually fall into bed with, and whom I would never leave.

The creative writing department at Concordia was nothing like UBC which, for all its flaws, had a basic aliveness and light. Most grad classes took place in the evening, which meant for much of the academic year we left in the dark. People arrived for classes and disappeared. There were few central spaces to gather outside of the classroom, other than bars (and there still aren't many). There were few gestures toward community building (there are more now). Little sense of care for students at all (every year now there is more). Administrative faces peered out and then sunk into retreat. When I failed to track down the man who was supposed to advise me (he lived in the townships and rarely came in, they said), the one who was instead assigned to advise me waved me into his office with the kind of grin of the front man in a low-rent cover band. He sat at the desk – relatively unused from what I could glean – in jeans and a denim jacket, like a nine-year-old dangling his feet and sucking on what appeared to be a Slurpee.

Isn't Montreal great, was the gist of his offering to me.

Yes, I managed, it is, but I was interested in how to best use the opportunity of the MA experience at the university to help me create a literary life.

'Oh yes, you'll find that on the Main,' he said. The Main? 'Yes. Saint Laurent,' he said.

'A literary life?' I asked.

'Oh yes,' he said, 'it's everywhere … '

'I meant something … more substantial,' I said.

'You mean, to find work?'

'For a start … ' I was looking for experience editing –

possibly work on a literary journal, or teaching, something that would help me create a life of the mind.

'For a woman who wants to write in this city you can't do better than serving drinks on the Main. That is what I advise all my female students.'

I blurted out that I thought I had made a mistake coming to this program and I was planning to go home in any case.

'Really?' he said. 'Because there's nowhere else on Earth I would rather be than right here in Montreal, living on the Plateau.'

In *AROOO*, Woolf spends ten pages trying to understand men's anger. I've spent more than a few dozen years trying and, in the end, I feel it has largely been a waste of my time. A few years back, several of my colleagues (mentees of the very man-boy professor I am now describing) were behaving inappropriately and no one seemed particularly concerned even when it was pointed out. I wrote a piece called 'Do Not Argue, Do,' in which I suggested that doing was better than arguing. I wrote this for many reasons, but, like most of the decisions I made in the early years of my time as a professor, I did it to illustrate what I thought was the most productive way to deal with the situation at hand: stop living in reaction to sexism and conservative criticism and create alternative worlds. I worked toward that in my classroom, and in the reading series I curated, and in my work.

I did – and do – feel resentful that it falls to women to tend to men's anger: to avoid it, work around it, soothe it, challenge it. Part of why I allowed myself to be seen as bitter in *My Ariel* is that I resented how many of my students had to do this work: to speak publicly over and over again about the misconduct of peers in the literary world and in my own university, where they wrote letters and finally, very directly, one of them wrote an essay describing the way her professor abused his power, manipulated, and used her.

I resented the silence from my colleagues. I resented that the students had to make these early years of their career about speaking to the culture that was impeding their literary growth in the first place. I resented having to carry the weight of childhood sexual abuse in my own creative space. I resented the fact that all this sexual misconduct had re-opened many wounds that I had spent many years working through. And some of those years in these very halls and classrooms.

Of course, it was presumptuous of me to try and speak for the young women. They have their anger and want to vent it how they want to vent it, and I need to take responsibility for how I did or did not vent or speak out about my own anger when it was me in their position. That's what I can do.

Still, my instinct is to put the anger back in my male colleagues' court. I want to sweep it from my room. I want my room to be light and healing. I want my room to be open to the freaks, the outsiders, those who fall through the cracks of intellectual success. Melodrama and bitterness be damned; bitter is a Venus flytrap for the feminist who lets down her guard. Like Sara Ahmed's figure of the feminist killjoy, who finds herself alone in the blue light of indifference, which only makes the bitter root reverberate more deeply and, as they say, 'no forms but twisted forms' can come from that, I am weary of twisting my body to move around the patriarchy and all its conventional, white tendrils.

Page after page of anger. We are due page after page of our own anger.

Some critics say Virginia Woolf's sophomore novel *Night and Day* is an answer to her husband's own sophomore novel. It presents a cast of largely unlikable characters examining the rituals of dating and the business of marriage and the use of rooms – domestic and otherwise – and questioning their purposes. There are many heated discussions between the potential couples; what is clearly being crafted is an unconventional marriage of equals. Significantly, too, *Night and Day* marked the end of Woolf's literary dependence on her half-brother, Gerald Duckworth. Starting with her third novel, *Jacob's Room*, her own press, the Hogarth Press, published her novels and so, truly, she did not have to worry about the critic.

It took her another ten years to reach her stride. According to Leonard Woolf in *Downhill all the Way: An Autobiography of the Years 1919–1939*, the turning point in Virginia Woolf's writing career came in 1928, when she was forty-six years old, having published five novels and reams of criticism. With the publication of *Orlando*, which sold 8,000 in the first six months in England and 13,000 in the Americas, Woolf, for the first time in her life, 'succeeded in earning as much as 545 pounds from her books in the year – the most that she had ever made before was 356 pounds in 1926' (L. Woolf 143–145). According to Leonard, this was twice the sales *To the Lighthouse* saw in an entire year.

The week after *AROOO* was published, in October 1929, the stock market crashed, launching the Great Depression and the long road to World War II. Despite this, *AROOO* sold 12,443 copies in England and nearly 11,000 in America in the first six months. *The Waves* followed in 1931 with over 10,000 sales in America and the UK; *Flush* did equally well. Her most successful, sales-wise, was *The Years* – in Leonard Woolf's words, 'much the most successful of all Virginia's books' but also, in his opinion, 'the worst book she ever wrote' (145).

I notice that when I am describing my ideal room to people, it often shifts between the two: on the one hand, yes, I want a place where I can sit and think. But I also want a place where I can move. I imagine this room as beyond constraint. A studio with light, on one hand, and space, and colour, and on the other a space with books and a desk, a chair by the window, and a garden that plunges into the room, or a room that plunges into a garden. I imagine a door that opens from my chest leading to a pond, from the pond to a perennial garden, through my lungs to a Japanese garden with a hill and a Thuja, rock, sand, a pool; the garden that surrounds my cabin becomes gardens, like the dreams I have when I am feeling confined or constrained by a project: a room that opens onto other rooms that opens onto other rooms.

For much of the past decade I have not had a room with a door, but I did for a time have a closet under the stairs. Then, just before the outset of Covid, I took a room at the back of the house. All through lockdown I worked on and in that room, making it a place I could write this very book, while also dealing with the noise of twin nine-year-olds who ran up and down the hallway between Zoom classes. When I first looked out the large window, all I could see was a wrought-iron spiral staircase, a very worn fence, and beyond that my neighbour's red brick walls and matching staircase. I planted a large white hydrangea, and over the years, coaxed vines that I now curl up and around the spiral staircase.

When Woolf was writing a novel, Leonard writes, her room became chaotic with its 'filth piles.' We have this idea of her perched in her opulent writing room: the image most often circulated is of the green bedroom she had added on at Monk's House, or of the Writing Lodge, which was also moved and changed.

But of course she didn't write only there, in the room she had built for the purpose of writing. The bulk of her mature work was written between Monk's House and the basement of the house at Tavistock Square, and there, as Leonard describes, the situation was squalid. Here's his description of the material, physical traces of her practice:

> With regard to her writing, Virginia certainly never learned to practice equanimity. Like most professional writers, if she was well, she went into her room and sat down to write a novel with the daily regularity of a stock-broker who commutes every day between his house in the suburbs and his office in the neighbourhood of Throgmorton Street. Her room was very different from a stockbroker's office. She was an untidy writer, indeed an untidy liver, an accumulator of what Lytton Strachey used to call filth packets, those pockets of old nibs, bits of string, used cigarette-holders, etc., which accumulate malignantly on some people's tables and mantelpieces. In Virginia's work room there was always a very large, solid, plain wood table covered with 'filth packets', papers, letters, manuscripts, and large bottles of ink. She very rarely sat at this table, certainly never when she was writing a novel in the morning. To write her novel of a morning she sat in a very low arm chair, which always appeared to be suffering from prolapsus uteri; on her knees was a large board made of plywood which had an inkstand glued to it, and on the board was a large quarto notebook of plain paper which she had bound up for her and covered herself in (usually) some gaily coloured paper. (L. Woolf 52)

'The litter in this room is so appalling,' she writes in 1939 'it takes me five minutes to find my pen' (*Diary, Vol. 5*, 250). *Squalid*. Like Tracey's Emin's *My Bed*, and Jeff Wall's *The Destroyed Room*. But mess, and apparently noise, was not an issue for Woolf when actually writing. When writing, according to Leonard Woolf, she acquired a protective skin or 'integument' that 'insulated her from her surroundings.' Here he goes on to describe Virgina's creative process, her intense ability to concentrate – not 50 percent but 100 percent was the rate of concentration while she wrote. Discipline. Routine. Shifting from intense 'dream-like' stages, flung out into long walks, periods of distillation: the body and mind an instrument. I like to think about the idea of the room, which has been central not only to feminist thinking about a writing practice, but to most people's thinking. But the room, very often, comes to seem like a kind of enclosure, a container for chaos.

Poems are also enclosures. If a poem is a room, it too could be a place I might inhabit. A life of the mind then, could be a poem.

By the fall of 1993 I was thinking of the stream of poetry workshops I had moved through, beginning with Ron Smith at Malaspina. He had instilled in me respect for the word and the page and the craft. The deep work was what mattered – reactionary was only successful when one knew intimately what one was responding to. As for the self, it had to be a self 'laid over' or responding to another self.

According to my second professor, at UVic, poems happened in the home, in the kitchen, over dinner, while bathing your children. Poems could be upbeat, they could be ekphrastic – about art – or about historical figures. You could clip her poems out of a journal and put them on your fridge, she said. She also suggested we enter contests. There was never a time when a journal in Canada did not have a submission from her. She was always worried about me after reading my poems, so I had the feeling, always, that my poems were muffled.

My third professor, Daphne Marlatt, wondered why there was never an I in my poems. Why were they so nice? And who was I speaking to, because poetry is a conversation. This she illustrated by introducing us to her wide network of poetry interlocutors by way of their books and essays. Thinking was visible on the page. Thinking, not poetic form, or not only form, shaped the poems. The details were so private and intimate, who are these people in the poems?, I wondered. And how, if I did not know who they were, could I appreciate the poems?

My fourth poetry professor, at graduate school, had a regard for received forms and high lyric voice. Here we wrote sonnets, ghazals, etc. The literature course she taught on Canadian poetry was challenging and informative. It led to intense discussions about nature and technology, cyborgs and goddesses, the demonology of science, the question of who can speak for whom? We read Atwood's *Survival*, dissected her poems to see her relationship to nature and landscape, and Dennis Lee's *Savage Fields*. We read Michael Ondaatje's *The Collected Works of Billy the Kid* and thought about the use of documentary in long poems, and Christopher Dewdney's *Predators of the Adoration*, with its 'core sampling' and erotics of geographical histories. We read Dionne Brand's *No Language Is Neutral*, and her essay 'Who can speak for whom?' We argued about deconstruction and what made radical content. We compared the way Erín Moure upended a poem versus Lorna Crozier's prodding at false comforts.

The experience of encountering Moure in person in Montreal then was life altering. Like Jane Rule, she towered over us so that when she reached up as if to touch a birch tree that was a column of light in one of her poems, I felt the bodies around me brace as if the room had tipped and we were sliding out into the hallway and down the escalator.

> … Who won't see who. Who
> who is. The woman with brown eyes, & one with
> blue. She longs for her kisses, means who? Who

turned away? Whose curls? Her heart pounding over
Its edge? The written? (59)

Everything that Moure said hit like shots of adrenalin. It is
not, her poems asserted, the poet's job to be nice.

Whatever the flaws of my education were, the poets
brought ideas to the table. They blew my mind again and again.
And that, I began to understand, was what a life of the mind
could be.

Maybe, I thought, it's not so much about Woolf's notion
that we have to 'kill the angel in the house' (which calls up the
same violence I wanted to escape) as it is breaking the mirror
Woolf talks about – the mirror that traps women into merely
witnessing heroic action, or being acted upon, rather than acting
themselves. The patriarchy traps women into submissive posi-
tions in order to maintain the illusion of men as having authority
– no one knows this more clearly than young women who date
older writers or professors. Men become uncomfortable around
women they can't see themselves in. And women free themselves
when they stop allowing themselves to be used in this way.

This mirroring was often benign, but not only. I had grown
up with the nightmare of women's bodies showing up on the
roadside, dumped. It seemed extreme, but it had been with me
as a possibility since early childhood. Since the first prison escape
near my school, and the Green River murders, and in movies,
and on television. I learned to drive on the Highway of Tears.
Near toxic man camps. I worked in restaurants where they stayed.
And was harassed by them in the hotel where I worked. Being
fixed in their gaze could be literal, but also allegorical.

'What do you think you need?' Moira had asked me one day in
her office in Nanaimo. 'I need to be conscious,' I said. 'What
makes you think you are not conscious?' 'I am not in my body.'

'I have made an art out of avoiding pronouns,' I write in an unpublished essay on Erín Moure in 1993, 'they have been my enemy. I thought I could write the unwritten by excluding the parts of language that limited. I wonder how long it would have taken before the whole language would have gone?'

My father, who spent most of his life away, working with road crews, building highways through British Columbia, was often referred to as a man's man. He was firmly and proudly a working-class man. He was not interested in any of the trappings of masculinity: never watching or playing sports, for example, and to my knowledge he never sat in a bar. He rarely drank, in fact, other than Cointreau for a rare special-occasion Sunday brunch.

On a spring day in the parking spot outside the trailer in Terrace, a small town in the north of British Columbia, nestled along the Skeena River, my father popped the hood of my mother's old Chrysler Newport, pointing out parts of the engine, the dipstick, the oil filter. 'Why are you telling me this?' 'I'm telling you because I want you to know you can do this yourself if you want.' 'I don't think I want to do that,' I said. I didn't even want to drive. 'No, but you could. And if you are paying someone to do it for you, I want you to know what they are doing.' 'Well,' I said, 'I doubt I will need that.'

'What I want you to know,' he said finally, 'is that men hoard knowledge. They withhold it from women. They will sometimes be more intelligent than you, but not generally. The world is designed for people with a slightly less than average intelligence. You have at least average intelligence, therefore you should trust your instincts.'

Human consciousness is staggeringly uneven. Life has moments of clarity and generosity, and then moments of panic and cruelty. For example, when, later that same year, after a period when my mother had been particularly unhinged, requiring an excess of support, beyond what was already an unreasonable demand from a child, I begged this same father to let me go away to boarding school – as he had done – so I could take seriously my education. I was waking up to the cost of our domestic dysfunction: I had already failed Grade 11 English and was going to do so again.

How was this possible? I was at least, as my father had just affirmed for me, of average intelligence. And I was motivated. At fifteen I was already working two jobs: one in the hotel in town, the other working for the daily newspaper. Both jobs required me to start work at 6:30 in the morning. Weekends I worked in the hotel restaurant. Weekdays I was first to arrive at the newspaper office where I stripped the newswire service stories that had accumulated overnight, wrote copy, developed rolls of film and printed the day's photographs. I was a person deeply motivated and dedicated to becoming a writer and I was failing English.

What was confusing – and here I think about Woolf's observations early on in *AROOO* of legacies passed down from mothers to daughters – was how completely devoid both my parents seemed to be of concern for my education. My mother kept me home to sop up her sorrow, and for the comfort of my company. She never allowed me time to do homework. She absolutely did not care.

I suggested to my father that I would go to the convent that he and my mother had often threatened my sisters with, because my mother's emotional and physical demands were too much for me. I was her crisis counsellor; she would wake me in the night for support, and this could go on until morning. What she really wanted was my father, and what my father really wanted was a divorce. But he was Catholic, and so he simply held her at bay and continued to work out of town, coming home once a month at most.

'What do you mean, not letting you go to school?'

'Keeping me up all night crying, needing me to soothe her.'

'She doesn't do that,' he said.

'Of course, she does,' I said, 'the same way she does it with you.'

My father's fists came fast and hard in response, blackening one eye and splitting a lip. All his rage and frustration about his disappointing marriage, his body being caught up in cycles of capitalist labour, poured into my face and body. When he was finished, I had been knocked against the wall and slumped in the pile of shoes and tools in the joey shack attached to our trailer. 'You are not going anywhere,' he said, and abruptly left, driving himself back to wherever it was he had found work that season. A few days later I packed my own bags and walked out.

What my father illuminated to me – aside from the fact that the people we love can know better and do harm – was that there were kinds of knowledge to be had, and that summary and recitation was only one kind of knowledge, and violence was another. Further, that when we began to see through this flood of words, and began to hear and see the intention behind those words, and then act on them, and to ask for equal treatment – our share, of space, of access, of protection – we are often met with more violence. Even when the intention was good. The unmasking of privilege will always be met with violence. A violence of words. A violence of fists. A violence of being.

It seemed also, from my perspective, the hallmark of hetero-sexual marriage.

And it was as if my relationship with L. was marked as a success when we achieved a kind of violent passing, when together we found some echo of this way of relating.

This is the beginning of the end, I noted on January 2, 1993. I had bought my ticket to Montreal. But as time is not at all linear, I realized that I was already there.

Chapter Six

The light of the September morning rose up through an unmasked sky, the ever-present post–climate change wind tapping its furious messages by any available means: vines, branches, undergraduates, even the hems of schoolgirls leaving class. Several decades had passed in a wink. All the new varieties and strengths of weather, now upending cars, now swelling riverbanks, now creating domes that cook the air like microwaves – all of this we carry around in our veins as we move through the nearly post-Covid city.

Yes, I thought, Montreal was winding herself up again. Montreal, the post #metoo Feminist City, was astir: another election cycle, another academic year leaping into gear, all the full white rooms swelling at the gates. It was tempting, after all this reading (and writing), to look out the window and witness the Montreal taking place on the morning of the 11th of September, 2021, with a resignation borne of fatigue. I felt the twentieth anniversary of 9/11 as somehow continuous with Mary Beton rising up and looking out the window in the autumn of 1928, for I felt, suddenly, very close to Mary Beton, a fictional version of Virginia Woolf, and this version of myself in my own life, in my own city.

And what was the city doing?, I asked. Nobody, it seemed, was reading poetry. Montreal was wholly indifferent, it appeared, to Virginia Woolf. Nobody cared a straw – and I do not blame them – for the future of fiction, or the death of poetry, or the development by the average woman of a prose style completely expressive of her mind. If opinions on any of these matters had been chalked on the pavement as they are on Twitter, nobody would have stooped to read them, accustomed as they were by now to taking it all as a matter of weather to be moved through, forgotten as soon as it has passed, if indeed it was noticed – if it could be noticed under the bell jar of sound most people walked down the street in, trailing their one-sided conversations behind them. If not that, then surely the nonchalance of hurrying feet and young couples with bundled babies in strollers would have rubbed these words off the concrete in half an hour. Here came an errand-boy; here a woman with a dog on a lead.

The fascination of a Montreal street in 2021 – like the streets of London in 1928 – is that no two people are ever alike; 'each seems bound on some private affair of their own.' There were the businesslike (very few, it must be said, on avenue de l'Esplanade) with their little bags; there were the children rattling sticks upon wrought-iron fences; there were the returning students, thousands of them – all characters to whom the streets serve as theme park, Grindr app, pub, and living room.

The young passed on all variety of wheels from skateboards to unicycles; non-binary bodies in electric cars offered information about blockades in the forest and land defenders without even being asked. Also, there were funeral processions streaming past to which old-fashioned lesbians, thus suddenly reminded of the passing of their generation, lifted their caps. And then a very distinguished transwoman with an elaborately brocaded mask came slowly down a doorstep and paused to avoid colliding with a bustling young woman who had, by some means or other, acquired a splendid furry vest appropriately torn to reveal breasts tattooed with two swallows and a lotus flower. They all seemed separate, self-absorbed, on business of their own, having no more idea who was and was not vaxxed as one could ascertain which gender one had been, at birth, assigned.

Then, suddenly, at this moment, as so often happens in a city – though rarely, it seems, on social media – there was a complete lull and suspension of traffic. All held for several moments before a single leaf detached itself from the gigantic half-stripped maple tree at the end of the street, and in that pause and suspension, fell. Somehow the half-devoured leaf was like a signal falling, a signal pointing, not only to fall, but to a force in things which one had overlooked: the gypsy moths having arrived on the wings of Covid and, a mere eighteen months later, dug themselves into the forests of the city, upending its tunnels of shade. The leaf seemed to point to an old river, which flowed past, invisibly, round the corner, down the street, and took people and eddied them along, as the streams in old novels, which, like benign and kindly old women, carried time.

Now the leaf was bringing water from one side of the street diagonally to the other. The water was full of plastic, in which could be found, as if it were a game on an iPhone, lost objects – patent leather boots, a maroon overcoat, a taxi cab – click, click, the fluidity of the world refreshing in your screen.

⚜

How do I make a writing life? That's the question at the heart of all the emails, all the applications and raised hands in writing rooms, and one that I have been thinking about and hoping to answer in this text. How did I? But also, how does one? This is the question that waves of young women have in hand upon entering creative writing programs. It was on my mind long before I encountered Woolf in 1988, and when I moved from college to university, then to my cabin, and then to graduate school in Montreal, and on to Toronto, and New York. Those of us who are determined, those for whom writing is not an option but an insistence, we give our lives to writing. We fling ourselves at it again and again.

And yet in every room we enter we find ourselves at risk of being turned into a handmaiden to someone else's journey, fodder for someone else's fiction. Vanessa Springora's book *Consent*, in which Springora takes control of her own narrative, outlines how she was offered up to a literary pedophile who groomed and seduced the young girls he went on to have sex with and then to write about them and their sex, and which many audiences have, for decades, consumed with apparent delight.

That is an extreme case. Nonetheless, the condition is as pernicious as it is banal. The way a group of literary peers, for example, will assume that the white male genius at the core – and there is (or was, in my day) always a white male genius at the core – is worth all of their combined energy to keep afloat. For example, Woolf apparently decided on the sum of 500 pounds, not because it was her own income but because it was the minimum sum the poet T. S. Eliot would accept from his friends who wished to support him with an annuity so he could leave his job at the bank and pursue writing and editing full-time.

Imagine that happening for a woman? A group of peers deciding, early on in her career, that her thoughts were worth protecting? That they needed to gather together and buy her time?

Find a hungry young writer, a male colleague suggested to me early in my teaching career, a young woman, they will do anything for you.

I saw my own young self, leaning against his office door, waiting.

It's not rooms, or poems, I feel I'm negotiating this morning, it's ice floes. I feel as though I'm leaping from one to the other as they melt, and the water is rising fast. But why mix metaphors?, I ask myself. What have I accomplished with all these mixed metaphors? And why drag L., as I have, or Professor Norton (likely lining up for his pension now), or any of the old professors into this narrative? It's been more than twenty years since I left the West Coast, since L. and I broke up. She has had a whole other life … surely we have all forgiven each other, moved on?

Because I am trying to make sense of the rooms. And all the pressures of the rooms. And the defence of rooms. And the loss of rooms. And the way that we lock ourselves up in rooms. How do we keep our rooms? How to move through them without getting trapped? Why does love trap? Love, like the love the writer Elizabeth Smart had for her beloved George Barker, that kept her circling in his wake all her life, and the love Plath had for Ted Hughes that seemed to make her succumb to the patriarchy, and how I, too, nearly sank myself, thinking it was love (wasn't it love, in the end?). It was the feminist poet and scholar bell hooks who first made me see that what I thought was love wasn't love at all. Love does not have fists. Love does not require domination. Love does not require your silence. It can't be enforced by withholding, or threats and demands for loyalty.

Nor is love easy, though; my life, my work, is unthinkable without the woman I finally found and married, a woman I had to travel across the country to find, when I didn't even know I was looking, and for whom I had to carry on, taking risk after risk, in order to remain at her side. Which is to say that even when I finally found love it required such a long succession of rooms, and in each of those rooms a different set of negotiations, and each of those negotiations a different evolution of self, a bid for equal and engaged presence on a shared path.

Yes, a good marriage, as George Eliot, and the characters of Jane Austen knew, is essential to a productive life; can we say, in 2021 that what they were looking for was support? Or, that good relations are part of the equanimity we dream of?

In a twist of fate most uncommon in the history of female literary genius, it is not Virginia Woolf's novel-writing career that ends with marriage, but Leonard Woolf's. Virginia had a breakdown shortly after marrying Leonard Woolf and spent the next three years, as she says, 'in a mad house.'

My younger self was always angry at Leonard Woolf, and the narrative we lesbians told ourselves in the 1990s, when finding out who was queer was an ongoing preoccupation, was that of course Woolf was queer and would have been happier living with a woman. That may be true, but even then I wasn't entirely convinced about the happier part. In my experience, queerness had in no way protected me from violence. So far, at least, it hadn't created a productive space.

I fumed through DeSalvo's account of the Woolfs' marriage and Leonard's spiteful novel, *The Wise Virgins*, which he began on their honeymoon, drafting a world in which his alter-ego rejects the fictional portrait of his wife. But what interested me was Woolf's own account, late in life, looking back, with calm pride, on the thing she and Leonard created. Also, snippets of negotiations in progress. On the publication day for Vita Sackville-West's *The Land*, and in the middle of the editorial process for Hogarth's publication of Sackville-West's *Passenger to Tehran*, Woolf records an argument she and Leonard have had just as she is wrapping up *To the Lighthouse*. The scene is a dinner party at Monk's House, the argument, she says, Vita started by coming over with someone who seemed not to have been invited and 'L. [I say] spoilt the visit by glooming because I said he'd been angry. He shot up, & was caustic. He denied this, but admitted that my habits of describing him, & others, had this effect often.'

In the vivid prose typical of her diary entries, Woolf moves from this scene to self-reflection: 'I saw myself, my brilliancy, genius, charm, beauty [&c. &c. – the attendants who float me through so many years] diminish & disappear.' She follows this with a harsh description of herself as 'elderly,' 'dowdy,' 'fussy,' 'ugly,' and 'incompetent.' 'I saw this vividly, impressively,' she concludes, as if letting the image simmer for her reader as much as herself. Then, she writes, 'he said our relations had not been so good lately' (*Diary, Vol. 3*, 111–112). The clarity with which she confronts Leonard here on how he treated her socially, publicly, was familiar, and exhilarating to me. Every social event of my twenties was followed by a long list of reasons for self-recrimination and embarrassment for my social awkwardness and a sense of largely being at odds with most of the situations I found myself in. I was constantly in a muddle about where I went wrong, and what was the proper behaviour to expect from myself, or others for that matter. There is also, no doubt, jealousy on Leonard's part, seeing Virginia fleshed and flushed out by Vita's physical love (their own union being sexless). But, nonetheless, here Woolf sees it all with enviable clarity and expresses it directly.

Then there's the marvel of her awareness of the impact of criticism on her self-image, and her self-awareness:

On analyzing my state of mind I admitted that I had been irritated, first by the prevalency of the dogs 'grizzle on heat too.' Secondly by his assumption that we can afford to saddle ourselves with the whole time [*sic*] gardener, build or buy him a cottage, & taking the terrace to be garden … Too many women give away on this point, & secretly grudge their unselfishness in silence – a bad atmosphere. (112)

'Too many women give away … ' – as I have done on more than one occasion, perpetuating this power imbalance in relationship after relationship. Here Virginia Woolf acknowledges and rejects this tendency. Then she goes on to narrate the impact of her husband's treatment of her: the spiral into self-loathing that chases away her well-cultivated self-caring thoughts, which she regains to set the terms of her domestic life – also how she wants her future to unravel, which is to say, to not be overly invested in the exterior of their home by over-spending and overwork. Finally, she gets to the crux of it:

… we shall be tying ourselves to come here; shall never travel; & it will be assumed that Monks House is the hub of the world. This it certainly is not, I said, to me … L. was, I think, hurt at this, & I was annoyed at saying it, yet did it, not angrily, but in the interests of freedom. (111–112)

We also see how she has, as always, at the centre, her desire for intellectual freedom. She doesn't always achieve what she sets down here, but she is always aware of the interrelatedness of the work, how it is bound up in all the other things she is juggling. She writes 'on analyzing my state of mind' and then goes on to give a sober account of her mind and body. It's a somatic encounter, allowing her mind to connect actual events with what had, at the outset of her account, been more free-floating feelings. This is a remarkably empowered relationship to the self.

But as we know, her self-awareness – in and outside of her marriage – is hard won. She began the previous entry for Wednesday, September 15, as follows:

> Sometimes I shall use the Note form: for instance, this
> *A State of Mind*

Woolf then goes on to give a much more intense and dire account of her mind:

> Woke up perhaps at 3. Oh its [*sic*] beginning its coming – the horror – physically like a painful wave swelling about the heart – tossing me up. I'm unhappy unhappy! Down – God, I wish I were dead. Pause. But why am I feeling this? Let me watch the waves rise. I watch. Vanessa. Children. Failure. Yes; I detect that. Failure failure. [The wave rises]. Oh they laughed at my taste in green paint! Wave crashes. I wish I were dead! I'm only a few years to live I hope. I can't face this horror anymore – [this is the way of spreading out over me]. This goes on; several times, with varieties of horror. (110)

The second entry reveals, yes, a sentimentality, but also great intelligence, emotional bravery, and sharp instinct; here she is panicked, but she stays the course, she does not look away: 'There is an edge to it which I feel of great importance … one goes down into the well & nothing protects one from the assault of truth … ' (112). Either way, there is tremendous strength in not turning away, and in this act, not of self-harm, but of self-care, she can begin to accumulate the strength she'll need to stay the course for her major works, still ahead. The sister books *Orlando*, *A Room of One's Own*, and *The Waves* make clear the complexity of the terms of creating her writing life: that handling her marriage, her domestic scene, her literary scene, her self, owning her own means of publication, and tending her family networks were all vital, as was the garden, but so too was the love of Vita, the final ingredient in a carefully tended creative life that made Woolf's three towering books possible.

Writing didn't come together for me as a viable and healthy practice in my life until well after my graduate degree, which I completed in 1995. The program was a rough diamond. On the one hand, it accepted many applicants (such as myself) who would not have had access to graduate programs otherwise. There was a distinction between the English and Creative Writing streams in the department: the writers accessed both streams while the English students did not. The difference in our experience was subtle but important to those of us looking for ways to realize a writing life. As my adviser made clear to me, writing lives were not about the university. The general vibe then was that it was the bar, the informal gatherings, where the real learning happened. I avoided male professors, taking all my creative writing workshops with women.

Several students I met through the department – Margaret Webb, Kathryn Mockler, Trish Salah – remain my most valued friends. The greatest gift from this time, however, was my partner, who is writing in the room adjacent to me as I write this line. We are all looking for a room to hold us. We are all looking for some kind of equanimity: immersive, independent, yet connected.

⊼

At the height of her career, on March 28, 1929, with the proceeds of her own writing – in the single biggest earning year of her life – Woolf notes in her diary that she wrote to

Philcox, the local carpenter at Rodmell, and began discussions for a writing room of her own.

Two rooms in response to *AROOO*. It's a luxurious situation. But when the Woolfs moved into Monk's House a decade earlier in 1919, there was still an earth closet (outhouse) in use: over the years, much work had already been done. Including work on the writing lodge – a story as important to the development of Woolf's work as the indoor writing room at Monk's House and the basement room at Tavistock Square. It was, I believe, leaving Asheham and arriving at Monk's House just after the First World War and at the tail end of the Spanish flu when Woolf began to dream, not only of the space of the garden and its proximity to her writing life, but of getting her mind and body as much inside the garden as possible. She tried sleeping in the lodge, she writes to her sister in 1928, but it was too uncomfortable and cold.

Inspired by her writing, and her relationship to herself, I imagine, but also by Vita Sackville-West, who was a serious gardener and had published *The Land*, a georgic filled with gardens and sentimental language, which won prizes and sold many copies, and for which Woolf had little respect, Woolf scribbled the design of two rooms, stacked one upon the other: one for sleeping and one for writing.

I have never been in these rooms myself, but I hear that one must go out of the main house to access this indoor writing room, though it is attached to the house. I don't know the exact details of how she entered and exited, what she saw, how she moved, but I love the idea of having to exit to enter.

By this time, Woolf had been writing for a decade in the writing lodge at the end of the garden. That too evolved. In 1934 – because of noise – she had the writing lodge dismantled and moved to the back of the property, near a wall with a view of the downs. In this iteration, the roof's peak changed for reasons that are unclear to me. At the start there were windows in the peaks above the doors, and in the end, there is only roof. There, on summer afternoons, the light moved straight through the lodge, and we see photos of Woolf and friends assembled in low chairs in the summer, reading. So, the writing room was central, and also social, and always evolving.

Nuala Hancock notes in her excellent book on the subject of Vanessa Bell's Charleston and Virginia Woolf's Monk's House that the two sisters, two incredible centres of creative power, were a bicycle ride apart, each of them a kind of testament to the power of a female, work-centred domesticity.

Wherever she went, Woolf was triangulating. And in a way, that tendency started at home.

It's a mistake to consider the room without all of its entanglements. Yes, one wants a door that will lock. But one also wants food, and to have the bed made, and so on. Domesticity is a key to any successful writing life. Our own pandemic has brought this reality into sharp relief. As did the pandemic for Woolf.

Looking at the two Decembers of the Spanish flu helps illustrate this. In 1918, a strand of influenza comes up vividly in Woolf's household. In December 1918, Vanessa Bell is getting ready to give birth and the Woolfs are to take Bell's sons, Julian and Quentin. In a volley of letters back and forth concerning milk, absent pocket handkerchiefs, and reading materials, Woolf offers an account of their first night at Asheham, when the Woolfs' servant, Nellie Boxall, is woken by a second servant, Lottie Hope, and in turn wakes the Woolfs: 'It was rather marvelous, considering that we were roused at 12.20 by Nelly [sic] with the news that Lottie thought she was dying.' They find Lottie 'in a state of hysterics for no reason that we could discover except that she felt very cold, and thought she had influenza.' There is an account of them settling her down and reassuring her by taking her temperature with a broken thermometer and gaining peace. But Lottie goes on to wake Nellie again the next night, who in turn wakes the Woolfs again, and the disruption carries on. Much is made of these ongoing disruptions in Woolf's journals and correspondence, but without much empathy; as Alison Light points out in *Mrs. Woolf and the Servants: An Intimate History of Domestic Life in Bloomsbury*, Woolf is always describing their maids at a distance, and as if they are children, upsetting the type, losing objects, interrupting. A quick scan of the index of Woolf's published diaries for entries related to Nellie draws a compelling portrait from volume two alone: 'infested'; 'declares herself dying'; 'taken worse'; 'never to recover'; 'her vapours'; 'still diseased'; 'healthy in all but teeth'; 'threatens cheap meal'; 'presents ultimatum'; 'will stay on'; 'moping but loyal' …

The December affair is clearly the result of an accumulation of stresses as we, who are now living through our own pandemic, might recognize. Combing back through the journals and letters, I see that on April 5, 1918, when the epidemic is peaking in England, there are many visitors at Asheham – always a point of tension between Woolf and Nellie. Lytton Strachey stays on, remaining in bed for twenty-four hours, very ill. When, later, Lottie describes his 'green sickness' to Woolf, she is repulsed not by the account of the vomit, or the fact that it is Lottie who will tend to and clean up after her guest's illnesses, putting herself at risk of possible contagion, but by Lottie telling her the details. Then there was the matter of a neighbour dying of influenza in the summer, and ongoing guests and stresses.

Both Lottie and Nellie are exhausted and terrified of becoming ill themselves. As domestic workers, they, like the thousands in America who were let go without any support when the Coronavirus hit in March 2020, were entirely dependent on the generosity of the Woolfs in sickness and in health. When

Vanessa's children appeared, it was never going to be Woolf who fed, washed, and cared for them. It was Lottie and Nellie who went to market, Lottie and Nellie who were constantly exposed, and whose work multiplied with the extra bodies.

A similar accumulation of stresses occurred in 1919, culminating, on November 28, with Woolf noting that Nellie had given notice after a period of eight days in which they had 'three dinner parties and two tea parties; and Angelica Bell, aged 11 months, and her nurse come to stay … ' (*Diary, Vol. 1*, 313).

But Nellie does not leave, and the second December, the first in Monk's House, ends with Woolf suffering a bout of influenza, which in her diary she describes as a 'low kind,' but which was likely, Elizabeth Outka argues, the Spanish flu. At the same time Leonard is ill with malaria, and it is the labour of Nellie and Lottie that sees them through nearly two weeks of combined illness.

Domestic space can be a powerful creative space for women – but it's not good when we accept (and contribute to) the gross imbalance of wealth and power. Woolf knew that. Here, in one of a string of moments in which Woolf struggles with her position in the household, she writes, 'our domestic system is wrong.' It is the system that leaves two young women 'chained in a kitchen' who must 'laze & work & suck their life from two in the drawing room … ' (314); it is the system that gives Woolf her position in the drawing room, and, she realizes, it is this system she will have to come to terms with if she is going to create a sustainable (and ethical) writing life for herself, and peace with Nellie and Lottie. Indeed, at one point she notes that if she were reading her own diaries some years on, it would be her relationship with Nellie that she would look at with greatest interest.

'In the midst of my profound gloom … one sees a fin passing far out,' Woolf notes in her diary in September 1926 (*Diary, Vol. 3*, 113), as she begins to ramp up the thinking that will culminate in the trio of books, *Orlando*, *A Room of One's Own*, and *The Waves*, that for me make up the true core of Woolf's vision. The fin, like the churn at the core of Beckett, a vision of the sensation of embodiedness: that is the core of Woolf, great compassion for the state of being human. If I close my eyes, I see bodies tumbling through time. I see many bright colours, textures, pleasures, sounds – it is a bacchanal of sensations, her vision. And through it she stitches a firm line.

Having accepted and soothed her domestic situation as best she could (she never really resolves it; even when Nellie finally leaves, she still requires domestic labour) and being already immersed in London, and in literature, Woolf now needed to be immersed in Nature.

The first mention of *The Waves* in her letters appears to be January 9, 1929, in a letter to Vita who had opened for her vast rooms of creative potential. In her diaries we see that the moths that are at the core of *The Waves* had been flitting in and out of her diaries since 1925, but I see them flitting as early as 1918 and 1919, during the First World War and the Spanish flu epidemic, when she is forced to consider in yet another light the interdependence of all bodies to thinking.

To do this, to truly feel others, she needed total immersion in the city, hence the walking routes, famously mapped out in *Mrs. Dalloway*, but already present in *Night and Day*, where the characters peer in windows and try to assess the suitability and gender of rooms, and what might be done in them. But immersion in the city was also not enough. Woolf's privilege meant that she grew up steeped in city life, but having summers at St. Ives, so she knew instinctively, and no doubt expected to continue to have a hold in the country – in the nature of the garden, in any case. Only after Woolf has achieved this total immersion in her garden do we begin to hear the thrum and interplay of human and biological consciousness first glimpsed in diary entries during the pandemic. Architecture, war, and lockdowns, it seems, can open us up to this. Here, from an early section of *The Waves*, in which I believe it is Rhoda speaking:

> Now I will walk, as if I had an end in view, across the room, to the balcony under the awning. I see the sky, softly feathered with its sudden effulgence of moon. I also see the railings of the square, and two people without faces, leaning like statues against the sky. There is, then, a world immune from change. When I have passed through this drawing-room flickering with tongues that cut me like knives, making me stammer, making me lie, I find faces rid of features, robed in beauty. The lovers crouch under the plane tree. The policeman stands sentinel at the corner. A man passes. There is, then, a world immune from change. But I am not composed enough, standing on tiptoe on the verge of fire, still scorched by the hot breath, afraid of the door opening and the leap of the tiger, to make even one sentence. What I say is perpetually contradicted. Each time the door opens I am interrupted. I am not yet twenty-one. I am to be broken. I am to be derided all my life. I am to be cast up and down among these men and women, with their twitching faces, with their lying tongues, like a cork on a rough sea. Like a ribbon of weed I am flung far every time the door opens. I am the foam that sweeps and fills the uttermost rims of the rocks with whiteness; I am also a girl, here in this room. (72)

As critics – Lauren Elkin in *Flâneuse: Women Walk the City in Paris, New York, Tokyo, Venice, and London* and Francesca Wade in *Square Haunting: Five Writers in London Between the Wars* – have pointed out, Woolf was unmoored by the loss of her London home during the second of the world wars she would endure. There are gripping images of her walking into her home in October 1940 to find broken glass several inches deep on the floor: 'I cd [*sic*] just see a piece of my studio wall standing: otherwise rubble where I wrote so many books' (*Diary, Vol. 5*, 331). After retrieving some possessions, they returned to Rodmell (Monk's House) for good. There she could walk on the downs – with some stress, as that area was a flyover for German planes – but she could no longer walk through London, something she had continued to do with great pleasure through the First World War and the Spanish flu epidemic, and for the first few months of the Second World War.

Woolf's productivity relied on a great many things, from the 500 pounds a year to her class and relationship with her domestic help, to Leonard's evenness, the luck of real estate in both London and Rodmell, the depth of her familial roots in the English literary canon, her ongoing relationship with her father in her writing, her dedication to critical writing, her relationship with the TLS and the creation and tending of a public critical voice, and, most importantly to my mind, the fuelling of a tendency toward always triangulating her perspective to keep a whirling, well-aired centre in her mind where the flames were always reaching up and her thinking was always full roar. And how she influenced us!

In a recent dream, I am in a small room, like the room I slept in with L. in the hollow, with the green floor, just big enough for a bed, with one small window that banged open onto a fir tree.

Paul B. Preciado, the errant French writer, and Virginia Woolf are in bed with me. Preciado – whose gender is far in advance of our own moment, let alone Woolf's moment – is electric, and I think we are both longing to seduce him. Woolf is thin and a tad brittle. She understands I am fond of her and will tolerate me as I lie in between them like a stretch of pudding. They must converse over me. Preciado is lobbing questions at Woolf: What good is a room if you're alone in it? And she is responding: Or if it looks like a catalogue? What good is it if your room is apolitical? Or if it lacks art? If the room is for parties? Hats? Fashion? Conventional genders? What good are sentences, he asks, if you can't ride them? Fuck them? Unlock all the doors with them? Let everyone out!

All I can think of is that I would like to be ravished the way that I first felt ravished by *The Waves*, and *Orlando*, but now Preciado is lighting Woolf's cigarette, their elbows painfully splayed on my breasts (why do you still have those? That's a chapter of its own), and I realize that while I've been thinking that they have already begun and ended their affair. They peer at each other as if somehow they are two halves of a whole, and exhale. Desire, of course, is another necessary aspect of a writing life. And there is nothing slack in Woolf's sentences; they are, like Orlando's hounds, always pulling the reader forward, forward, threatening to upend or devour.

'As for the mot juste,' Woolf writes Vita Sackville-West in March 1926, 'you are quite wrong. Style is a very simple matter; it is all rhythm. Once you get that, you can't use the wrong words' (*Letters, Vol. 3*, 247). Sackville-West's poems proceed with buckets of confidence and mere echoes of rhythm.

The scenes I loved best in the 2018 movie *Vita & Virginia* involved Woolf in the pressroom: Woolf striding through the bustle of machinery and ink to her writing room. The activation of making.

As for sentences, they are like small poems. Which is to say, why bother if when you get to the end you are merely where you began?

Here one comes to the matter of the peroration, which convention demands, and while I am not a fan of convention, I am a fan of Woolf (by now a fact overstated), and as such the peroration is in order. I have tried to account for my relationship to Woolf, to writing, and to rooms; to the debt I owe her work, particularly AROOO, which, I believe, has everything in it for contemplating the making of a writing practice.

I have, I hope, illustrated that on the surface there is the room, the 500 pounds, but at the core is a free, intellectual life. Further, that the desire for a room of one's own is an unsettling, guilt-inducing desire, particularly at this time when we have all been in forced isolation in rooms – many of which are woefully inadequate – and when so many of us still don't have basic necessities, or even a room, let alone a room of our own, and when so many of us have had many rooms of our own for a very long time and have never worried about whether anyone else has one too, which is to say, in our society, a room comes generally at the expense of someone else not having one.

The desire for the singular room is both understandable and vexing – *why?*, some of my male colleagues say, incredulously, as if their right to a room and time to think is as divine as the right of kings to rule, both in terms of resources and sustainability. Which begs the question: what does one actually *need* in material terms to be able to write once, as Woolf suggests, we remove (if ever we truly can) the always aggressive gatekeeping of white patriarchy?

The question of the room, and the continuous securing of the room, and the income, is ongoing. In the morning, I walk by the women on the bench outside the shelter down the street, smoking, their bags at their feet, staring into their phones: they themselves are the only rooms they possess in that moment.

Some women are rooms that other women long to inhabit. Woolf is a room. Is a portal. Make of yourself a portal, I tell myself, make your classroom a portal.

In a room at Hedgebrook, a retreat on Whidby Island, I lay awake reading notes from other women who had slept and worked in the same little cottage. *The fridge is too loud*, writes a grumpy Dorothy Livesay a decade earlier, *I can't sleep!*

I sleep next to women in other cabins; we cross paths in the bathhouse, share our work after dinner in the living room of the main house. Women like Pramila Jayapal, who would later become a Congresswoman and the first South Asian American woman elected to the U.S. House of Representatives, and my dear friend Phebus Etienne, who went into enormous debt to attend NYU to work with Sharon Olds, and then left us, far too young, her beautiful collection of poems grieving the loss of her overworked, underappreciated mother largely unpublished.

The future is always unknown, but for most of western civilization it has least been an imaginable continuation of something resembling the present. Woolf wrote *AROOO* at the height of her literary success, and right in the middle of the twenty-year period between the world wars. It was a brief moment of security. She also wrote at times when bombs were falling on her head.

We are at a moment where we can't fathom even the possibility of a future some days, let alone what it might look like. Even those of us who have sought to create a new reality – to break down the systems of life that have made so many rooms uninhabitable for women, indeed for so, so many – seem to have been caught off guard. Those for whom the pre–Covid-19, pre–climate crisis world was already a dystopia, are also caught off guard.

Many of us who have been stuck in the status quo, no matter how forward we thought our thinking to be, circle ourselves, incapable of seizing the opportunity to realize the change we dream of, and which would be useful to fulfill in this moment. But still, it seems, we are hemmed in by convention. We are still thinking of rooms as having four walls. A window. Stable weather. A view. We hope for a view. We are, in the end, too easily pleased.

I marvel at the millennials, who have opted not to tolerate. They are creating new orders. They are not accepting the status quo. I am grateful for the Black women radicals and Indigenous resistance who are fighting to upend racist colonial structures. That is where the rooms I want to inhabit are aligned. I don't want a room on the space shuttle, on whatever trajectory Bezos or Musk create, or in communities built by the realtors grabbing property in all the urban centres they rightly assume will be the safest destinations in the climate-changed world to come.

No. Those are not the rooms I dream of. Any vision of the future I will fight for will come from struggling youth.

But how, Woolf asks, facing the enormity of the questions she has unearthed, how can I further encourage you to go about the business of life? In all this chaos? And for us, the new, endless chaos?

In light of all this, one must ask, what is the right relationship of room to our time? Of writing to life? Young writers, as Woolf says, please attend. I have some statements to offer:

A room full of women lock arms and begin to move the room toward higher ground.

They hold tight and whip themselves forward, toward the sun.

If you consider your house a body, I hear Renee Gladman say, you won't be surprised to find that a house moves.

The room high above the city, or the room below ground – here I am again, at the apex of my living, in one of these basement rooms. I look up onto the dark garden where, by trial and error, I have found the shade plants that work and tucked them into pockets of earth; like the women, they stretch and tend toward the light. The light is a window, the light is out into the world, the witness; the plants are a ladder that leads my eye to a possible future. Equinimity is flexible. So, too, a room.

Is that practical enough? Perhaps some images of the future?

I dream of a honeycomb of rooms, one for each of us.

A room that reminds you that you are not one in *a* million; you are one *of* millions.

Don't make of your body a bulldozer.

Don't make of your mind a fence.

I break out into poetry to find a way through. A way through is poetry.

A billion rooms-of-one's-own or none.

The dream of the room is a boat.

The women circle. They are in and out. They are fluid.

The dream of the room is the core dream. The root dream.

A room, alone in isolation, a room in relation to isolation's rooms.

Is any room other than the room you are in, in relation?

Don't wear your room on your sleeve.

I wear my room on my sleeve.

Please, dear women, wear your rooms on your sleeves, but by now aren't we sick of the word *women*? And all that the word leaves out? Including myself. I do not feel myself in that category. Can we not renovate the word?

For many years now I have been in the habit of renovating spaces (and texts!) I am in – or want to be in – in my mind. What room would be the best enclosure? Thirty years on. I dream of a studio at the edge of a wood, or a bucolic version of Monk's House, but built on reclaimed industrial land. I walk down the street imagining my room and how it will be. I amble through a novel imagining what my version would be. Maybe this is from my time with L.? The potential for built space? For creating something inhabitable. Durable. A text for others to enter and relax in. What will the reader feel in my spaces? What will they see?

    I also reimagine public spaces. I reimagine streets and blocks. I open the backs of the triplexes on the ruelles I walk along – in a city that has so much winter and so much light, the design of the buildings on the Plateau is mystifying. The house fronts are in side profile to the sun, they are long and resemble the trailers I grew up in, which resembled, in turn, coffins, closed in, turned away from the city. As I walk, I imagine the backs of these triplexes opening out onto the laneways – many of them blocked to traffic and given over to vines, cats, and children who run up and down them in all seasons. The future arrives – including the many monied young couples vacating real estate–devastated cities elsewhere to cherry-pick this city and modernize the old structures – like a wind, and waves me off.

But why? Now I'm irritated. Why is the future waving me off? Or have I misconstrued the gesture? Is it because I am a not woman not man? A not-man-not-woman woman? A not-woman not-man ? I am not the butches I came to queerness through. I am not the femmes. I am not trans. I am a not femme, not butch, not trans queer. I am androgynous. I am fluid. Non-binary. I am what I am.

Woolf says there must be unity of mind to create great writing. Maybe there has to be unity of mind to simply be? In any case, of all the difficult gifts the millennials have offered, pronouns are my favourite. And now, having been given the gift of pronouns – of course I am *they*, not *she*, or *he*, I have never been *she* or *he*, I have always been something in the middle – I see myself coming down the road. This is long past gender. Long past the primacy of heterosexuality.

I wish I had half the confidence of Eileen Myles, who is happy to declare themselves the gender of Eileen Myles.

My hair turned white the year Covid appeared. My hair circles my head like a wreath of comic exclamation marks.

If my body has gained any intelligence, it is that it is and has only ever been marginally female but also that it is not at all male, nor with any desire to be so.

I look in the mirror and see myself emerging. My gender is like a sign I hold in the wind; it is changing, changing, changing. It is as fluid as a mood.

Walking through a post-hurricane Red Hook a few years back with friends, I could see the water at eye level: all the new builds with their first floors empty and fitted with flood gates for the water to flow through when it comes; the IKEA up on pylons with parking underneath. Yes, I think, lift and turn; I see the old factories lifting up and stepping back from the sea that for so long we took for granted, that for so long we thought only carried us and bathed us and brought us dinner as we walked along the placid length of its seams.

I imagined a writing room on stilts, walking into the forest. A house with skirts that can stand when the weather is good and squat over the garden like a giantess, enclosing it between her legs.

I miss the old weather.

I am sure the animals, too, miss the old weather.

I am sure the trees, too, miss the old weather.

And the dinosaurs must miss the old feminism too.

We have known about climate change – the public, I mean, not the scientists – for thirty years, I think, feeling the salt of Woolf's peroration, and I have had her books in hand for thirty years, and I have achieved so much, and still I do not feel unburdened, still I am not disentangled from the bogeys I came through, the view from here is still uphill.

Communally we have had Woolf's wisdom for a century. There's no future without communally. It is a single dream-house vision and a larger, more nefarious corporate grab of rentable space that we're up against. The future wants us to own nothing, and not in the way that the Trotskyites dreamed. The future wants us all to rent from the rich. We'll inhabit a little blind spot in their mind.

Meanwhile, single dream home after single dream home goes up in the countryside around a lake I love.

'I don't want a room if there are no like-minded people in and around it,' my partner says. 'What good is a room without people?'

Don't think about retreat, don't think about bolstering your own windows, think of the city's windows, the city's rooms, think of the polar bear's room and the fox's room, and the baby cougars and coyotes and the butterfly routes and the goldfinch and the deer.

Can we build caves in the mountainside for them to retreat to? Can we create diversions to ensure water flows more evenly through the forest?

Cut carbon and adapt. The dream of the room is a net-zero room. The dream of the room is less is more. A zero-carbon footprint of one's own.

Don't talk to me about downtown revitalization, talk to me about moving water around, under, and through rooms. And not only my own.

A walk in the world is now a walk of mitigation, because it is so hard to imagine anyone giving up their privilege to make the necessary changes: Why should I be the one to pay the tax of adaptation? Why should I be the first to give up my car? Why should I be the first to go *zero waste* in my kitchen? Why should I be the first to do what I know needs to be done?

You will remember, some time back, the ongoing dreams of the man with the knife? And you might ask whether this is a story that ever ends? Well, there was an end to that sequence of dreams.

It occurred in the room I lived in while finishing my MA, under the apartment of my future partner, while I was writing my thesis, 'Someone from the Hollow.' I was trapped in a basement full of plastic. It was rising all around me, like the water in *The Poseidon Adventure* – the scene where Shelley Winters has to swim from one section of the overturned boat to the next to help free those trapped was marked indelibly on my childhood – but it wasn't water in this dream, it was, I could now see, doll parts.

Then I heard the familiar scraping of the knife at the window and there he was, the figure of all my nightmares, knife in hand, slipping like a draft through the window. I knew the drill and began swimming as hard as I could, but soon my arms were hitting the ceiling.

As with my student's dream, it felt as though this dream cycle was neverending, that there was no way out of being triggered and traumatized. Finally, I reached the stairs, which I leapt up three at a time. He was already behind me, gaining. I leapt and leapt, turning a corner, then up another flight of stairs, turning a corner, then another, and a corner and another and, finally, I thought, *No. No more.* This is what I had been willing myself to do. To stop and turn. Which I did: I stopped and turned. I could hear him coming. *Now,* I said, closing my eyes, *I need two big, thick, massive doors.* I could see them vividly and when I opened my eyes, there they were. But so was he. *No,* I said again, reaching up and calmly slamming the doors shut. *Now,* I said, *I need a massive wooden bolt.* And there it was, as thick as a thigh. I reached up and slammed it down across the doors. I could feel his body slam against the other side. But nothing. Nothing. I knew there was no continuation of this scenario. I could feel it. I turned, exhausted, to find three ancient figures, sitting calmly around a table, watching me.

'Welcome,' they seemed to say, motioning me to join them, 'welcome.'

News of my thesis, 'Someone from the Hollow,' came over the phone: two yay, one nay. 'I suppose that means I'm doing something right,' I note in my journal in June 1995: 'if everyone loved it, I'd have to wonder.' The defence date was set for a few weeks later. My supervisor had been supportive, if hands off. She found my work, she said, 'deeply moving … beautiful poetic narratives of wounding and survival.' She was a yay. I had not met either of the men who served as readers for my thesis prior to my defence: Professor N. was a yay, Professor B., a nay.

The abstract of my thesis describes the work as a journey divided into four sections – 'childhood, rites of passage, coming of age and coming to consciousness' – and notes that 'the poems are meant to capture the natural process of memory as well as narrating one's life story; they are meant to have a fractured quality, while maintaining a larger narrative structure. I have attempted to overlay experiences and perceptions of specific events to illustrate the effects of trauma on an unconscious level, and then attempted to make these connections conscious … '

The defence began with a preface by Professor N. detailing the hostile early reception of Walt Whitman's *Leaves of Grass*. Professor N. went on to describe my thesis as flawed but 'bold, venturesome and complex in technique.' He then offered a thorough reading of its strengths and weaknesses. Professor B., on the other hand, described me as a writer who 'disdains poetic form and rhythm as well as the language of poetry.' Further, that my thesis 'might well be autobiographical snippets and jottings [that] deliver dreary, platitudinous, and trite chitchat' and it failed 'to demonstrate mastery' of either poetry or prose. The interrogation proceeded at length. At one point, frustrated with my inability to explain myself to his satisfaction, Professor B. yelled, 'I have daughters, their lives were nothing like this!'

Professor N. argued for a list of minor changes that could be made that would surely satisfy Professor B.; Professor B. argued that not even major changes could redeem the work since it was not poetry. My thesis supervisor, who would later become my colleague, said, maybe he's right? At this point the defence seemed to collapse and, exhausted, the professors agreed that I would make 'Major Changes.' I was sent home with a list.

A few weeks later, on my thirty-second birthday, I received a fax. It was titled 'Reader's Reconsideration.' Here Professor B. explained at length that he had reconsidered his position based on the defence and several re-readings and that he must accept the work 'as is' with no changes, noting

The narcissistic preoccupations of this persona – , if there are mama-boys in the world, this is surely a mamma-girl speaking – , its pathetic self-indulgences and clichéd female chauvinism, besides boring me, do not accord with my experience of young girls growing up – and I've raised three of them and am friends with them all – is not relevant to an assessment of the candidate's writing skills, but to her maturity as a writer and that is not for me to judge.

In short, I had achieved what I had set out to achieve and done so with 'admirable skill.'

The following year, after thirty years of teaching, Professor B. retired. My flawed and raw thesis remains, bound in red, on the shelf in the library of the university where I returned, more than a decade later, to work. And still do.

But I never could shake the sting of the defence. I could not 'unhear' the descriptions. I was at a dinner with theatre people around the time I got news of the 'reconsideration.' The other women there had a terrific laugh. 'Consider it a badge of honour,' they agreed.

Later, my play at SummerWorks received a *Toronto Star* review that described my character as a 'menacing self-obsessed lesbian.' My partner cut the headline out and made a badge with it that I wore for the remainder of the play's run.

These events have a way of reverberating through one's life. They are, as Hawk Owl, my therapist in Nanaimo, had warned me, impossible to dislodge. But they must be resolved. And apparently resolved again and again and again. A few years after I returned to work, Professor B., having retired the year after my defence, contacted me, in my capacity as organizer of the reading series, asking if I would invite him to read from his latest book, a collection of poems about his childhood trauma.

⚔

For years the ending of my last nightmare was a relief.

Now when I do think of the three figures, I realize that they are unstable. Sometimes I have remembered the figures as women. Sometimes genderless. Sometimes I see that there is tea. Sometimes not. And why do I say they welcomed me? They have never offered me tea in my mind, or moved to soothe me, they barely even turned to acknowledge me. They were just there. Not quite startled; expressionless, really. So what does it mean to be welcomed? I think this may be a symptom of the problem of mentorship my generation seems to have had. Or my own unease at being mentored. And the difficulty of being a mentor myself.

How did I want to be welcomed? What would it have meant to turn from the momentous moment of ending my long nightmare to find open arms? *How great that you have succeeded! Come, let us hold you while you cry!* How did one ask for help? How was one soothed? How does one welcome and soothe?

Three figures in women's mythology would surely be crones, and that is what I assumed, but I see now that they are not crones at all. They are androgynous figures, and they are encased, trapped in layers – of what? Disappointment? Resignation? Hard expectation? They had always been very still, not leaping to my aid, not animated. Now I see they are stuck. Cold. Lifeless. Frozen out of time.

In my waking dream, I rush over to them and rub their shoulders and backs, blow into their faces. I feel the cold of their bodies, encased in something like concrete. I dig and dig until I have torn my nails. There are no tools on this landing, where I have been in mind so long, like the tumour ticking behind my third eye. So I begin to bite and gnaw and tear, and finally I reach skin, beautiful skin, and an aliveness that glows from within the encasing. I realize I am standing in concrete rubble. I am not too late. Not too late at all. I carry on knocking the concrete to the ground, rubbing the arm, and the shoulder, and then the head, very gently uncovering the body.

There is no water, nothing there at all, and I am tempted to start licking like a dog licks the wrist of its human companion, waking them from a long, dangerous sleep – one that had perhaps ensured their survival through a turbulent time, but whose numbness, and layers of protective coating, have now become a kind of shell in which they are immured, and in which they can hardly breathe, and which certainly it is no longer necessary to remain inside.

I feel similarly about rooms.

Having, over the past three decades, dreamed of achieving and creating a room of my own, I realize that, like Woolf and her room (or rooms), the room itself is truly not the point. Yes, it would be lovely to have a writing lodge as Woolf had at Monk's House, where one has the pleasure of crossing space – a garden, preferably – to enter it, or to have a space in the home with a door that locks, a door that blocks sound, and moreover someone, like Leonard, to bar people from entering it. Also, a flourish of people with the desire to enter the room in the first place. But if I've learned anything in my long journey to writing and my long search for a room of my own, it's that it isn't as easy as the 'if you build it, they (the books) will come' mantra. A room doesn't write a book.

Still, one dreams of a particular room. And with that room, a particular quality of mind. A better frame of mind, if I'm honest. On some level I believe this room to be intrinsically linked to realizing my potential. And I'm not alone in this. The Internet is full of images of writers' rooms, shelves, and desks. Writers obsess about their rooms. My room! Where is my room? When will I have my room? In fact, I spent the early weeks of writing this very book thinking of the room and its value (practically and imaginatively) to women's writing while creating and obsessing over the room I moved into at the start of Covid, the room I thought was my own – a room I have already lost. Ceded, really, to one of my ten-year-old twins who used to come and lie on the carpet at my feet in the early mornings of Covid home-schooling while I tried to keep working, and thinking, about Virginia Woolf and my early relationship with her.

Was this room ever really my own? I was alone in it, technically, but as I said, the twins slid under the door while I blinked and then my students arrived, peering at me in the backdrop of my room (eventually I changed the backdrop to Vita Sackville-West's writing room), and then faculty arrived for meetings, and suddenly my room was just another space in which to serve. No, the room is an important idea, but it isn't the answer. Of course, it's complicated – it's time, and money, and confidence to express one's self no matter the backlash. It's a need for solitude, for idleness, and above all the ability to take one's thoughts seriously, despite ongoing critiques – necessary and unncessary – but here I was again, coming up against the desire, and resistance to the desire, for retreat. Whatever it is I am after, I thought, remembering the three static figures in the hallway, it isn't fixed in either space or thought. It may be a destination, if not a state of mind.

As Woolf realizes throughout *AROOO*, writing can only happen inside other writing, but also while rooted, and outward looking; it can write against, in spite of, or in support of, but it's always in relation. Writing continues writing. As for the room, for the frame of mind, for the space, well, that is an elusive balance. Somewhere between retreat and community there is a space. Not the classroom perhaps, nor the corridors where women's ambition lingers, often trapped outside the very rooms they dream of inhabiting. Like a series of connected buoys. Links in a chain. An adjacency. Like my ever-growing shelves of books by and about and engaging with Virginia Woolf.

Woolf describes this in *AROOO*, the gift of perspective. Once, having broken out of the room, one begins to find one's thoughts out walking – on the streets, yes, but also in libraries, classrooms, boardrooms, senate chambers. One sees oneself in all of these spaces. The more spaces, the more one's mind expands. One sees oneself in relation to so much more. One triangulates one's day: taps a string in the writing room, walks to the library, taps the string there, walks to a café, a park, a cinema and taps the string there, gathers wool all along the way – faces opening up like blossoms – and expanding, expanding, allowing more and more into the mind and onto the page. All the rich connections. One can't tunnel down until one has filled one's mind. It's a way of triangulating one's perspective and, in that way, deepening and widening and making oneself available and vulnerable to so much more life.

I bump up against something here that I have not had enough of as a writer: joy. The joy of that creative movement through the world. I do know it. But how does one navigate personal joy at a time of so much global pain? Here I feel more akin to the Woolf of 1939 than the Woolf of *AROOO* writing out of the last gasp of the 1920s London life. Having untangled these knots, though, I tell myself, I won't go back to joylessness.

We find in our genius foremother the ill-gotten gains of her colonial perspective, we balk at the problematic relationship to race and class, and the anti-Semitism she reveals in relation to her husband and his family. I take a cue from the scholar Terry Castle's 'Desperately Seeking Susan,' a devastatingly arch portrait of Susan Sontag, published not long after Sontag's death, in which, after a long ramble of admiration and skewering, Castle lands on a bit of advice from Sontag herself in relation to Virginia Woolf, which Sontag offers (in Castle's version of the event) harshly to her young acolyte: to judge a writer not by her worst work – in Sontag's estimation this is *Orlando* – but by her best. I would add to that, her best attributes. Dear reader, judge her by her best attributes.

About *Orlando*, I don't know that I agree, but I like how the example of Castle's relationship to Sontag here complicates what we expect of our heroines. They are flawed. We are flawed. We may not have burned off all the impediments of our early lives, our coming to our voices through violence – we may, some of us, never burn off the anger. In a way, I think of Woolf as my barometer.

Perfection has never been the point of loving Virginia Woolf, it has always been pleasure, and map-making. Her room is my room. My room is your room. I see a long line of writing moving forward through waves of linked individuals. Connected. Not as in the metaverse, and not on the screen, and, for sure, not only on the page. I see forms, interlocking arms, pools of time buoying us. Determined. Fluid. Ready. Receptive, not only reactive, but proactive. Ever undoing the knots of pain we inherit. Ever creating space for new minds to take root. That is, to me, the future.

Works Cited

Brand, Dionne. 'Who can speak for whom?' In *Brick: A Literary Journal*, no. 46 (Summer, 1993): 13–20.

Cusk, Rachel. *Coventry: Essays.* New York: Farrar, Straus, and Giroux, 2019.

DeSalvo, Louise. *Conceived with Malice: Literature as Revenge in the Lives and Works of Virginia and Leonard Woolf, D. H. Lawrence, Djuna Barnes, and Henry Miller.* New York: Dutton, 1994.

————. *Virginia Woolf: The Impact of Childhood Sexual Abuse on her Life.* Boston: Beacon Press, 1989.

Elkin, Lauren. *Flaneuse: Women Walk the City in Paris, New York, Tokyo, Venice, and London.* New York: Farrar, Straus and Giroux, 2017.

Gruber, Ruth. *Virginia Woolf: The Will to Create as a Woman.* New York: Carroll & Graf, 2005.

Gubar, Susan. *Rooms of Our Own.* Champaign: University of Illinois Press, 2006.

Hancock, Nuala. *Charleston and Monk's House: The Intimate House Museums of Virginia Woolf and Vanessa Bell.* Edinburgh: Edinburgh University Press, 2012.

Hardwick, Elizabeth. *Seduction and Betrayal: Women and Literature.* New York: Random House, 1974.

Hussey, Mark. *Virginia Woolf A to Z: A Comprehensive Reference for Students, Teachers, and Common Readers to Her Life, Work, and Critical Reception.* Oxford: Oxford University Press, 1996.

Morrison, Toni. 'Virginia Woolf's and William Faulkner's Treatment of the Alienated.' (MA diss., Cornell University, 1955).

Moure, Erín. *Sheepish Beauty, Civilian Love.* Montreal: Vehicule Press, 1992.

Outka, Elizabeth. *Viral Modernisms*. New York: Columbia University Press, 2019.

Poole, Roger. *The Unknown Virginia Woolf*. Cambridge: Cambridge University Press, 1995.

Rooke, Constance. *Fear of the Open Heart: Essays on Contemporary Canadian Writing*. Toronto: Coach House Press, 1989.

Rosenbaum, S. P. *Women & Fiction: The Manuscript Versions of A Room of One's Own*. Oxford: Blackwell Publishers, 1992.

Sackville-West, Vita, and Virginia Woolf. *The Letters of Vita Sackville-West to Virginia Woolf*. Edited by Louise DeSalvo and Mitchell A. Leaska. First ed. New York: William Morrow and Company, 1985.

Stape, J. H. *Virginia Woolf: Interviews and Recollections*. Iowa City: University of Iowa Press, 1995.

Woolf, Leonard. *Downhill All the Way: An Autobiography of the Years 1919 to 1939*. London: Hogarth Press, 1967.

Woolf, Virginia. *The Diary of Virginia Woolf: Volumes 1–5*. Edited by Anne Olivier Bell and Andrew McNeillie. First American ed. New York: Harcourt Brace Jovanovich, 1977.

———. *The Essays of Virginia Woolf, 1925–1928*. Edited by Andrew McNeillie. London: Hogarth Press, 1986.

———. *The Letters of Virginia Woolf: Volumes 1–6*. Edited by Nigel Nicolson and Joanne Trautman. First American ed. New York: Harcourt Brace Jovanovich, 1978–1982.

———. *Moments of Being*. New York: Harvest, 1985.

———. *Night and Day*. New York: Restless Books, 2019.

———. *On Being Ill*. Ashfield, Mass.: Paris Press, 2002.

———. *A Room of One's Own*. Edited by Mark Hussey. Introduction by Susan Gubar. First ed. New York: Harcourt, 2005.

Acknowledgements

I am indebted to the International Virginia Woolf Society, the Virginia Woolf Society of Great Britain, and the many Woolf biographers and scholars, especially Mark Hussey, Nuala Hancock, Julia Briggs, Alison Light, Emily Kopley, S. P. Rosenbaum, and Hermione Lee. Special thanks to Adrian, proprietor of The Word bookstore in Montreal, for helping me fill out my collection of Woolf and Bloomsbury titles. A SSHRC grant helped support research assistants, including Deanna Radford, Alisha Dukelow, Emma Cullen, Katherine Abbass, and Bridget Huh. I am grateful for their excellent work. Please see www.womenwritingwoolf.ca.

I dedicate this book to the many students of creative writing – undergraduate and graduate – that I have had the pleasure of working with and learning from over the years, and to all students, teachers, and administrators who challenge the status quo, for those who know, and insist, that the university can and must do better.

Love and roses to Coach House staff (James, Tali, Crystal, Sasha, Lindsay!), and to my editor, Alana Wilcox, for her belief in the work and for her intuitive and generous editing.

Endless thanks to Naomi and Sam for their penetrating perspectives and capacity for joy, and to Danielle, who makes everything possible.

From here to equanimity.

Sina Queyras is the author of *My Ariel*, *MxT*, *Expressway*, and *Lemon Hound*, all from Coach House Books. They were born on land belonging to the Nisichawayasihk Cree Nation and live and teach in Tiohtià:ke (Montréal).

Typeset in Arno and Didot.

Printed at the Coach House on bpNichol Lane in Toronto, Ontario, on Zephyr Antique Laid paper, which was manufactured, acid-free, in Saint-Jérôme, Quebec, from second-growth forests. This book was printed with vegetable-based ink on a 1973 Heidelberg KORD offset litho press. Its pages were folded on a Baumfolder, gathered by hand, bound on a Sulby Auto-Minabinda, and trimmed on a Polar single-knife cutter.

Coach House is on the traditional territory of many nations, including the Mississaugas of the Credit, the Anishnabeg, the Chippewa, the Haudenosaunee, and the Wendat peoples, and is now home to many diverse First Nations, Inuit, and Métis peoples. We acknowledge that Toronto is covered by Treaty 13 with the Mississaugas of the Credit. We are grateful to live and work on this land.

Edited by Alana Wilcox
Cover design by Ingrid Paulson
Interior design by Crystal Sikma
Author photo by Danielle Bobker

Coach House Books
80 bpNichol Lane
Toronto ON M5S 3J4
Canada

416 979 2217
800 367 6360

mail@chbooks.com
www.chbooks.com